The Hope of Heaven

The Hope of Heaven

GOD'S EIGHT MESSAGES OF ASSURANCE
TO A GRIEVING FATHER

BY ALAN M. HALLENE JR.
WITH ERIN KEELEY MARSHALL

NELSON
BOOKS

An Imprint of Thomas Nelson

Published in Nashville, Tennessee, by Nelson Books, an imprint of Thomas Nelson. Nelson Books and Thomas Nelson are registered trademarks of HarperCollins Christian Publishing, Inc.

Published in association with the literary agency of Books and Such Literary Management, 52 Mission Circle, Suite 122, PMB 170, Santa Rosa, California, 95409.

Interior design by James A. Phinney.

Thomas Nelson, Inc., titles may be purchased in bulk for educational, business, fund-raising, or sales promotional use. For information, please e-mail SpecialMarkets@ ThomasNelson.com.

Unless otherwise noted, Scripture quotations are taken from the HOLY BIBLE: NEW INTERNATIONAL VERSION®. © 1973, 1978, 1984, 2011 by Biblica, Inc. Used by permission of Zondervan. All rights reserved worldwide. www. zondervan.com

Scripture quotations marked CEV are from THE CONTEMPORARY ENGLISH VERSION. © 1991 by the American Bible Society. Used by permission.

Scripture quotations marked MSG are from *The Message* by Eugene H. Peterson. © 1993, 1994, 1995, 1996, 2000. Used by permission of NavPress Publishing Group. All rights reserved.

Scripture quotations marked ESV are from THE ENGLISH STANDARD VERSION. © 2001 by Crossway Bibles, a division of Good News Publishers.

Scripture quotations marked NASB are from the NEW AMERICAN STANDARD BIBLE®. © The Lockman Foundation 1960, 1962, 1963, 1968, 1971, 1972, 1973, 1975, 1977. Used by permission.

Scripture quotations marked NCV are from the New Century Version®. © 2005 by Thomas Nelson, Inc. Used by permission. All rights reserved.

Scripture quotations marked NLT are from the *Holy Bible*, New Living Translation. © 1996. Used by permission of Tyndale House Publishers, Inc., Wheaton, Illinois 60189. All rights reserved.

Cataloging-in-Publication Data available through the Library of Congress

ISBN: 978-0-7180-2205-1

Printed in the United States of America

15 16 17 18 19 RRD 6 5 4 3 2 1

To God, who joined me as a fellow grieving Father on the worst day of my life. You showed me that you understand because you also lost a Son. Your kindness, approachability, and omniscience assured me then that my son is secure and happy for eternity, and you continue to strengthen me with the hope that I will see him again someday.

Also to my three "Yellow Roses of Texas"—my sons Yalex, Bryboy, and Jimbob—and to Mom and Dad

Contents

1. One Day to Someday 1

2. Heaven in Minnesota 11

3. Our Time . . . His Time 21

4. The Gift of Life 33

5. Matters of Life 55

6. God Is a Dad Too 73

7. On the Bridge to the Other Side 85

8. Reason to Hope 97

9. Giving Alex Back 109

10. Hope Beyond Depression 121

11. Until We Meet Again 139

Notes 161

About the Authors 163

Chapter One

One Day to Someday

But you, LORD, are a shield around me, my
glory, the One who lifts my head high.
I call out to the LORD, and he answers
me from his holy mountain.

PSALM 3:3–4

*I*n the dark, early hours of October 2, 2008, my oldest son, Alex, left a message on my cell phone. So few
words, but ones that changed my life forever.

I missed the call, his last to me, because my phone was
charging in the living room.

He had left a message on my phone two days earlier, telling me how proud he was of me and that I was his hero. That
one had seemed overly loving, but this one made me shiver
as I listened to it later that morning.

"Dad, I love you. I'm sorry to let you and Mom down.
Good-bye . . ."

His words and tone set a host of fears churning in my
heart. Frantic, I tried several times to reach him. I even
called my other two sons, Bryan and Jimmy, but they hadn't
heard from him. So I rushed to my car and drove the three

hours from my home in Moline to our condominium in Champaign, where Alex was living while in his senior year at the University of Illinois.

I made the drive in two hours, barely able to breathe as I hurried to Alex's aid. It was a familiar journey. I'd traveled those roads countless times, many just in the previous months. Throughout that semester and the previous school year, I had made a habit of visiting Alex every other week or so to buy him groceries and fill up his Blazer with gas, really just to check on him. I knew he had been struggling with school pressures, but he seemed to be holding his own after a difficult time.

Never had the drive gone so quickly yet seemed so long. Even though I didn't actually know, I knew in my gut that he was gone. Everything in me wanted to get there, to see his smile and prove my instincts wrong, to listen to him laugh, to hear him say teasingly, "Relax, Al. What's bugging you?" This time, I promised myself, I wouldn't even get on him about the cigarette I imagined hanging from his mouth as he said it. Everything in me wanted to turn back the clock and demand a do-over, to shake off the tornado of dread inside.

Finally I turned in to the condominium complex, pulled in to the driveway, and ran up to the door. It was locked, but a note in Alex's handwriting was taped to it. *Do not enter!! Call Al Hallene.* He had added my cell number.

With a sinking heart I ran the stretch of front yards in the complex, then around the farthest one and through all the backyards to our unit. My emotions must have sent me into frantic confusion to sprint the length of a football field when I could have cut between two buildings.

Finally I stood looking into the rear picture window. The blinds were open, and my fears were confirmed. I was staring at my child's death scene. His body was hanging from a rope, obviously lifeless.

My knees buckled, and I went down.

I struggled to regain my footing and looked around for a planter or something heavy to shatter the window. But then I had a hunch that Alex had left the door unlocked for me. He had, so I ran inside and somehow lifted him up and removed the noose before we collapsed to the floor together.

As sobs wracked my body, I felt the stiffness of Alex's form. It was apparent from the rigor and the coolness of his skin that he was gone. Nonetheless, I tried a few rounds of CPR. He had been gone for hours, likely soon after leaving that late-night voice mail for me.

I held him and rocked him. It was all I could think to do right then. I bargained with God to let me trade places with my son, this young man with dark hair and features so like my own. His beautiful eyes that had gazed up at me in his first moments of life now saw nothing when I looked into them.

Minutes passed, then through my tears I noticed a small envelope on a nearby table. I managed to reach it and strained to read Alex's last words, scrawled in the familiar chicken-scratch handwriting family members had always joked to him about. *I'm sorry to everyone, especially my family. You guys were great. Please try to forgive me. I love you all.*

Those few poignant words reveal the essence of who Alex was: a great son and an excellent big brother who loved his family and cared so much for others that he regretted his act would cause us such grief.

To say that moment didn't make sense to me, well, the size of the understatement is sickly laughable. Nearly twenty-three years worth of learning and growing, laughing and disciplining, conversations about random happenings and big life issues, vacations and holidays, countless sporting events, tears and triumphs—all the things we enjoy with those we love, relationship minutiae we live without noticing—it was all gone. The pain of grief nearly choked me in those first minutes.

This son I cradled was the same fearless boy who had flipped over his bike handlebars, knocking out his two front teeth days before kindergarten began. He was the boy who fell headlong from atop the playground equipment and broke both his arms in second grade. Those arms had grown solid and muscular as he grew up; now they did not move.

Alex had battled on the football field, the tennis court, the golf course, the baseball field, and in the swimming pool—winning over and over again. He was supposed to win this one. He was born to win in life. He'd done it time after time, since his first moments out of the womb, with passion, grace, and laughter. Alex never gave up on anything and didn't back down from a challenge. His headlong rush through life made it seem all the more impossible that he was gone.

What I'd have given to see him sit up, to hear him toss attitude my way with a "Wassup, Al?"

He knew that would get a double take from me every time, and I'd respond, "Wait a minute, Alex! I'm your *dad*!"

Eventually grim reality set in, and I gathered myself to call my former Illini roommate and close friend Jim to help me by calling the authorities. I prayed that Jim, a successful businessman who traveled throughout the state, would be in town. As he has always been there for me at the moment I needed him most, he answered his phone.

I stammered into mine. "Jim, I'm at our condo. Alex had . . . a terrible accident. He's dead, and . . . I need you to call the authorities for me."

"I'll call them immediately. Jani and I will be right over." He must have known I couldn't handle questions right then.

I knew that shortly my private time with my son would be over. I had no clue how I was supposed to let go when the police arrived. How does one begin to let go of a child? Could I scream that question loudly enough to get an answer?

There aren't many singularly altering moments in my life, but this was one of them. Without warning, all my dreams for Alex felt lifeless. When he was tiny, I was his protector. To a large degree I, along with his mother—my former wife, Mindy—was in control of most things that affected him. The power of my influence on his life had been ripped from me, and I didn't know how to handle it. One act redefined so much. All I was capable of doing just then was to hold him and to grieve for all he, his family, his friends, the world, and I had lost because Alexander Montgomery Hallene was gone. Those thoughts rolled in chaotic waves.

All I really knew was how much I'd need God for my next breath, which came so hard beneath my weighted heart. I'd need him in the next hours as I sorted through how to tell Alex's mother and his brothers.

Then, in those ten minutes before Jim and the authorities arrived, a series of visuals unfolded in my mind that startled me with their clarity and power. They appeared in an orderly fashion despite the devastation. No doubt I was in shock, and yet I've always thought of myself as a levelheaded, boring engineer type, not prone to dramatic imaginings.

But on that worst day of my life, I experienced a series of miracles, or sensings, or feelings, all of them spiritual in nature, that have helped me to deal with the loss of my son. By nature I'm an outgoing person, but I don't tend to talk about something as personal as this experience. Still, since shortly after that day, I have felt compelled to do just that, even though dredging up the memories evokes great pain.

For a while I hesitated to share the eight messages I received in those ten minutes alone with Alex's body. I feared people might not take them seriously or might see them as mental fabrications induced by trauma. But ever since that afternoon, I have not changed my rock-solid certainty that

Alex is happy and safe, and I want others to have that same assurance of what awaits them and their loved ones after death.

This writing of mine is not intended to be some kind of everyman's guide to handling personal loss. My purpose is simply to share God's confirmation to one normal, non-flashy guy of an actual heaven and a living, loving Savior.

Today, several years into this sorrow, I can look back and recognize how much I needed the Lord ever present, not in the far-off way I'd always envisioned the Creator of the universe.

Those eight messages are still vivid to me, still comfort me, and still remind me that we all long to embrace the hope of heaven for our loved ones and for ourselves.

Are eight visual images enough to console my heart? No. But they are enough to give me a glimpse of what God has prepared for each of us. They are enough for now.

Chapter Two

Heaven in Minnesota

The LORD is my shepherd, I lack nothing. He
makes me lie down in green pastures,
he leads me beside quiet waters, he refreshes my soul.

PSALM 23:1–3

As grief and shock overtook me while I held my boy, a surprisingly real picture came to mind. As if a video were playing, I saw Alex and my late father ("Papa," to his grandchildren) in Dad's bass fishing boat at our summer home in Walker, Minnesota. They were wearing their safety vests and laughing and pushing off from the dock with their fishing gear, eager to catch "the big one."

I recognized the beautiful blue sky and voluminous clouds that sheltered our vacation cottage on Lake May. Over the decades, we'd spent countless days there together; it is still our family's heaven on earth.

As tears streamed down my face, I thought briefly that it was a fond memory of our happiest times together in what Dad had always called "God's country." He also liked to say, "No matter how bad things get, you can always go up to the lake, put a line in the water, and sort things out." I thought of how kind God was to give me that gift in my grief, until I realized that the scene was not a memory at all. It kept playing, as if in real time, with audio.

Gentle waves lapped at the boat, and I heard laughter from my father and son. I can't describe the magnitude of the warmth and happiness I felt. I do remember that it was more powerful than the grief for a brief time. And then, just as quickly as the image came to mind, it vanished.

But then another remarkable thing happened. Instead of lapsing back into despair, I understood that I had received a most unexpected and wonderful gift. I had been allowed to see and hear my two heroes again, happy and healthy, enjoying their favorite activity—fishing. I'd been given a glimpse into a current happening, right at that moment. But where was it happening?

I believe they were in heaven, not on top of giant clouds with harps playing, but acting as the vital, joyful people they had been during so much of their time on earth.

But as important as the message God sent was, I also believe he gave me the intelligence and faith to understand the certainty of it. It wouldn't have held such power without the ability to comprehend it. I'm not smart or creative enough to have thought this up, nor do I have special powers to come up with the only possible touchstone in my life that could, if only momentarily, blunt the tragic feelings I was experiencing. How vivid this scene still is for me years later. The clarity of my "video" remains amazing to me. It wasn't a dream or a conjured-up, hopeful happening. It happened. It was as if Jesus had given me a sneak preview of good things to come.

That scene at our lake home was the most effective one God could have chosen to communicate his peace to me. God had always blessed me with that Minnesota getaway, a place of thousands of happy family events over the years. It's our heritage, a place of ongoing life, of passing the legacy from generation to generation. My grandpa and grandma Hallene started going up there in the 1930s, and my mother told me I'd been there every year since I was a few months old. I'd continued that same tradition with my sons.

Alex and my father shared a special bond, which made seeing them together in that vision all the more meaningful. I remember one morning when Alex was a month old. We were living in Texas at the time, but we had traveled to the Quad Cities and were staying with my parents for Christmas. I woke up at six one morning to take my turn at feeding my boy. My father was up as well, and tears filled his eyes as he held his grandson. When I asked if anything was wrong, he proclaimed, "When your own child has a child, then you know life goes on."

Alex was the first grandson on that side of the family, and in honor of that position, my father gave him a red fishing boat that we all still refer to as "Alex's boat." In the image I received in the condo, Dad and Alex were in Dad's boat, but Alex's is still up at the cottage today.

Every year from the time Bryan and Jimmy were small until Dad passed away, they would ask him, "Papa, when are we gonna get a boat?" It became a family joke of sorts when they continued asking the question as teenagers.

Alex had a tender heart that grew ever larger as he did. After several hours of fishing one day, my dad brought his catch up to the house to clean. Little Alex was thrilled to be part of the action and sure that he could help prepare the flopping fish for eating. But as soon as Papa thumped the fish's head and made the first slice with the filet knife, Alex's brow furrowed, and he cocked his head. "Papa, do fishies cry?"

Papa had spent many hours helping all my boys learn to fish. One summer day he took Bryan out on the boat. Before long Bryan was working hard to reel in a whopper. He was hauling the big walleye up out of the water alongside the boat when it flopped one more flop, freed itself, and plopped back into the water. Bryan was crushed.

To add insult to injury, the next day my father went out and pulled up another whopper that, oddly enough, had a familiar lure and hook in its mouth. It was Bryan's fish that had gotten away. But Dad was the one to bring it home, so Dad's fish it was. It's mounted over the fireplace as his catch, a sight that hacks Bryan off every time he sees it. Pretty understandable; it is a beautiful fish.

No other place than Lake May holds such a sense of history and belonging for me. During tough times, I go up there and refuel and feel like myself, whole again.

As a family we celebrated many Fourth of July holidays there, which were a big deal in Walker. During the annual Independence Day parade, my sons and their cousins caught candy in our usual spot on the sidelines, kitty-corner from the Dairy Queen. My father often drove his 1931 Model A with the other antique cars along the parade route. Some one thousand people attended the festival of floats and exhibits, but the crowd seemed more like ten thousand.

My brother and two sisters often came to the lake with their families, and the atmosphere rang with fun, fishing, and golf at the nearby country club. The club owners even mowed a trail for us so we could drive our old 1960 Cushman golf cart from our cottage right up to the first tee.

Walker is a place of joy and family, of simple living where we avoid restaurants in lieu of grilling steaks or the day's catch right outside our back door while we watch the sun glisten on the waves as it bids us yet another good night.

Our final visit together at our summer home was a mere six weeks before Alex died. He and I and his good friend, also named Alex, traveled there together for one last fishing trip before cold weather and school stress set in. As had become my habit over the past months, during the trip I'd discreetly been watching for signs of how he seemed to be doing. He was laughing and appeared to be having a great time. The two of us even woke early one morning and fished alone together on Long Lake, a larger lake adjacent to May but one that we have many memories on as well. He was laughing and lighthearted. His friend Alex agreed with me later on that he saw no visible signs of distress in my Alex. I still wonder what was really going on in his heart, which he had become a master at masking.

Back in his Champaign condo, I wanted to stay in that carefree scene on Lake May. No, I wanted to *join* Dad and Alex where life's pressures melted away. I took the vision as a message from God that Alex and Dad were in fact enjoying a reunion someplace else that resembled our Minnesota heaven. They were together in the real heaven, and Alex was more than okay. He was healthy and happy, and I knew that his smile was genuine. He was no longer covering up hidden pain that we couldn't identify though we had watched for it so carefully during his last months on earth.

The emotional pendulum swung my heart from the anguish of discovering Alex's death, to the family memories, to the God-given peace of knowing my child was okay, just no longer on earth. I knew even then that God pulled me back from the lostness and steadied me with the understanding that my son no longer suffered.

That simple vision showed me God's unassuming methods of making himself known. He certainly communicates that way through my special-needs nephew, Matt. Tall and dark haired, Matt holds a special place in my heart. He and my boys grew up together, and Alex was a protector of Matt, making sure he was included and treated well.

Matt is my sister's son, who was born with a fragile X chromosome. It's a condition that makes him a simple man in many ways, but the rest of us could envy his strong faith. Innocent and good-natured at twenty-six, Matt doesn't possess great speaking skills, and he can't read. He lives semi-independently with a caregiver and loves to collect movies and toys that are appropriate for school-aged children.

In Matt's unique way of communicating, he expresses how much he misses Alex. A couple of times a week, Matt and I go out for ice cream or to a bookstore or a movie. Without fail, each time I arrive at his house he gets into the car and says, "I talked to Ah-icks last night."

Without fail, my heart quickens and I respond, "What did Alex say?"

"He said, 'Take care of my dad.'"

I see those words on the page, and I have to pause to let the meaning behind them sink in. I am not a theologian, and I am not here to debate whether people in heaven can communicate with us on earth. What I do know is that our Creator can communicate to us through whatever means he deems appropriate, and I'll leave it at that. I believe God is behind Matt's words, and his assurances to me through Matt are an example of Matthew 19:30 that the "last will be first" in heaven (CEV). There's a case to be made that the Lord has supreme blessings waiting in heaven for his own who have suffered on earth. Perhaps God's children who have an especially difficult time on earth will experience extra-special healing in heaven.

Matt is not surprised by Alex's words. Neither is God. The heavenly Father makes himself known to Matt on a level perfect for Matt's understanding, every bit as much as God communicated with me in a way I could understand on the day of Alex's death.

My memories and the Lord's constant presence carry me as I struggle to do more than survive these earthly days. I was given a chance to feel God all around and in me, and because of what he showed me, I believe I will see and laugh with Alex again.

I know that my Alex is waiting for me, and this knowledge gives me the fortitude I need until I'm with him again in heaven, with Jesus and Dad . . . and of course, big fish in a lake that looks like the one in our beloved Minnesota.

Chapter Three

Our Time . . . His Time

Surely your goodness and love will
follow me all the days of my life,
and I will dwell in the house of the LORD forever.

PSALM 23:6

*I*n the year or so prior to Alex's death, I—as well as his mother, Mindy—traveled often to Champaign to see how he was doing. That extra attention was prompted by an incident during the summer of 2007.

One night he and a friend borrowed my mother's car in Naples, Florida. They'd been drinking too much, and his friend crashed the car. Sick about it and feeling typically responsible, Alex cut his wrists soon afterward. I remember his phone call to me that night. He told me he loved me and that I was his hero and his best friend.

"Alex, where are you? It's not that big a deal. It was an old car. Besides, your friend did it, not you."

"Yeah, but I'm responsible."

"Alex, come on. Just tell me where you are."

Click.

That was one long and sleepless night.

The next morning Mindy called to tell me Alex had been found and he was okay.

We took him to a counselor with the hope of providing him additional support. He faced a measure of embarrassment from small-town gossip because the bandages on his wrists were visible to all. However, the psychologist didn't see the circumstances as an all-out attempt to take his life. The cuts were not deep enough, causing doctors to view his injuries as a cry for help.

Needless to say, Mindy and I still took the incident seriously, although we didn't feel a need to be terrified for his life. Instead, we visited often and offered support in every way we knew possible to help him heal. I frequently asked the hard questions about how he was truly doing, not just how he appeared to be doing. He understood I was searching for honesty, and he'd often answer, "I'm really doing fine, Dad. Really. I'm okay." I know Mindy tried to get to the heart of his heart as much as I did. But he had hidden the deepest parts of himself from us, perhaps for years.

Then, there I was, waiting for the authorities to arrive and take my son's body. I looked down at him in my lap, and sobs took over. Again I begged the Lord to let me switch places with him. I'd had a good run in my fifty-some years. Alex had his entire adult life before him. So much gone with one act of desperation, and I couldn't do anything to save him or bring him back.

Nothing could have proven to me more clearly than his death that I, as an earthly father, do not have control over my children. I had no clue how to begin processing my son's act to end his life. I ached over my inability to meet his needs at the most critical time.

I was baffled, wondering how I was supposed to fulfill my role in his life when my role had been usurped. I fought to reconcile the knowledge that I couldn't have done more to save him with my need to be the best father I could be. I couldn't understand why my love for him hadn't been enough to see him through his hardest times or why he didn't believe me when I validated his capabilities, when I assured him of his bright future, when I praised him for his many achievements. If I could clarify any of that confusion satisfactorily, maybe I could find peace.

But peace is not of this world and definitely not of human origin. If left to my strength, I'm certain I would have felt buried under the horror instead of carried peacefully through it despite my questions and confusion.

I'd been raised going to church, and Mindy and I had raised our boys in church. I knew God, or at least I thought I did. But he was revealing himself to me on his terms and in his way. In that small room that had been overtaken by sorrow and the destruction of human hope, I was for the first time meeting the Lord as he knows himself to be.

After the picture of my father and Alex came and went, I continued to beg God to let me trade places with Alex and return him to life. I knew that probably wouldn't happen, yet I was feeling swallowed up, and I thought anything could be possible.

I desperately willed the impossible to happen, if I could only pray well enough.

God didn't grant my request to return Alex to earth, but he did answer my prayer. In this second message, he quietly placed in my mind a long-forgotten Sunday school lesson. I guessed the words were from the Psalms, but I couldn't be sure. They began with something about the Lord knowing us before birth and knitting us in our mothers' wombs, and they were followed by something to do with the numbers of our days written in the Book of Life.

I recalled discussions in my Bible study group of scriptural passages that indicated each of our earthly histories was written in God's big black book even before we were born. I remember arguing that this couldn't be, that everything couldn't have been mapped out for us. How indeed, then, could we live our lives in our own free will?

I also remembered the discussions I'd had with God, asking why he allowed so many bad things to happen to innocent people. *What is the point?* I had wondered in my youth and, frankly, throughout my life. What was the point of trying to help others, of trying to raise a healthy family, of working hard and living a good life, when disaster could strike anyone, anywhere, anytime? Were there no heroes left to swoop in and save the day? I wondered why Jesus didn't come back and clean things up a bit, to help us mere mortals make sense of this mess.

Why try to make a difference if the apparently random

acts of life and of inevitable death made the plans of good men and women disappear? And all this came at the hands of a seemingly impartial, harsh, almighty judge who allowed evil people like Hitler and Stalin to destroy millions.

All my conjectures flowed as I hoped for my son to wake up. Those unresolved questions of my lifetime raged as I tried to focus on what to do next about Alex, about telling Mindy of our loss, as well as Bryan and Jimmy, his grandmother Mimi, and my brother and sisters . . . everyone who loved this gregarious boy.

Then a gentleness came over me again, as it had earlier with the vision of Alex and Dad fishing and laughing together. This peace warmed me, cleared out my uncertainty and budding anger, and gave me the resolve to find in the Bible those words that had just played through my thoughts. I needed to know how much God had already determined about Alex's days on earth.

Jumping ahead to the end of that long day, I finally had time alone around midnight to search the Psalms.

Psalms is not a short book. I can't help but think the length serves a purpose, because in trying to locate one section, a searcher often ends up browsing many other verses in the book, no doubt being blessed more in the process.

I flipped through 138 chapters, bolstered by the psalmists' wavering yet stubborn faith, reading about trials, losses, and heartaches, before finally finding the verses I sought. Psalm 139:13–16 says:

For you created my inmost being; you knit me together in my mother's womb. I praise you because I am fearfully and wonderfully made; your works are wonderful, I know that full well. My frame was not hidden from you when I was made in the secret place, when I was woven together in the depths of the earth. Your eyes saw my unformed body; all the days ordained for me were written in your book before one of them came to be.

A chill ran through me as I finished. *All the days ordained for me were written in your book before one of them came to be.* My weeping resumed. The Lord reinforced to me that he had indeed spoken to me, inaudibly as always, placing his words in my feeble mind.

Alex's death on October 2, 2008, was no surprise to God. He was not caught off guard. He was not feeling his own shock, but he was feeling mine with me. And he was letting me know that he had always been sovereign over Alex's days. Twenty-two years, ten months, and four days, to be exact.

Although suicide certainly wasn't in God's perfect plan for Alex, God knew all along that the day was coming when Alex would make a choice about his own death. I've got to trust that God made use of every moment to pursue Alex's heart; surely he sought out Alex even as the physical life drained from him, and I believe he welcomed Alex home to heaven because Alex had chosen earlier in life to give his heart to Jesus as his Savior.

God's words warrant taking the time to savor them, to

pull out every ounce of hope that he intended for us. Psalm 139:16 was such a verse for me from the moment I found it late that night. But as I have savored the whole passage since then, verse 13 stands out. No matter how hard anyone tried, no one could see into the deepest pained places of Alex. That's an agonizing thought to carry, until verse 13 reminds me that the Lord created Alex's inmost being. His Creator knew every crevice of depression that Alex masked before the seeing world.

The second half of the verse is equally loaded with peace. God knit Alex together before his mother and I ever met him. Consider the act of knitting. Each loop requires careful attention; each movement implies skill and creativity to make something beautiful and purposeful out of simple materials. Every motion in the process is precise, every inch touched personally by the crafter.

God doesn't toss a human being together, and he is not aloof toward his prized creations. He never once lifted his touch from my son—his son—even to the last moments that Alex's mortal body breathed. Even now he has not cast off Alex from his presence and care.

The bad decisions a Christ-follower makes do affect life on earth, and we'll face accountability for them in heaven (2 Cor. 5:10). But no one who seeks the Lord as Savior is ever lost to him. Romans 8:35–39 speaks clearly about God's power over anything that threatens to separate his own from him. This interpretation from *The Message* clarifies the eternal bond between a believer and the Lord:

Do you think anyone is going to be able to drive a wedge between us and Christ's love for us? There is no way! Not trouble, not hard times, not hatred, not hunger, not homelessness, not bullying threats, not backstabbing, not even the worst sins listed in Scripture . . . None of this fazes us because Jesus loves us. I'm absolutely convinced that nothing—nothing living or dead, angelic or demonic, today or tomorrow, high or low, thinkable or unthinkable—absolutely *nothing* can get between us and God's love because of the way that Jesus our Master has embraced us.

I think I could dwell forever on the comfort that God never gave up his stable hold on Alex, even when it appeared to Alex that his life was caving in, even in the hours of torment that he faced alone as he came to the final decision that the earthly struggle was too hard.

God held him fast. Nothing can remove the beauty of that truth. Depression and suicide are harsh realities, like so many of the world's agonies. But God's truth, love, forgiveness, and conquering plan for those who turn to him will always be greater. He can never be bested. And today Alex understands that his Lord never lost him. Because of Christ, we have the beauty of hope and healing that springs out of the very ashes that appear to bury us.

I knew my questions, sadness, grief, guilt, and waves of anger were not over. But my main concern regarding where my boy was right then had been answered. He wasn't in pain. He was joyful. Not merely happy, as he'd seemed on earth, but joy-full in God's glory. Despite my bargaining to have Alex back, deep in my soul I knew the answer. God had spoken to me silently and lovingly.

Alex was fine.

It's the rest of us who continue to cope with this pain we can't escape. I can cling to another truth in Romans 8 during low times. Verse 28 says, "And we know that in all things God works for the good of those who love him, who have been called according to his purpose."

The "And" at the beginning is key. In addition to his other assurances, God promises good from even worst-case scenarios. That's a truth to dwell on.

I have let the Lord draw me close to himself since Alex died. I've learned to lean in to him with each wave of sadness. I've run to him, in fact—oftentimes because I have nowhere else to turn if I am to survive this grief, but mostly because I long for the soul balm that only he gives.

Just as God knew Alex and knit him together before he was born, he knew and created me. He saw the days of my brokenness coming, and he was ready for them even when I was not.

As I held Alex, God held me, and he holds me still.

Chapter Four

The Gift of Life

I will remember the deeds of the LORD; yes, I
will remember your miracles of long ago.

PSALM 77:11

The birth of any child is a heaven-sent gift, a miracle. But when the longing to raise a child remains
unmet, as ours was for years, an extra-sweet thankfulness
flows when the miracle happens.

God's third gift to me after Alex's death was a consum-
ing gratitude that I had been allowed to parent him for nearly
twenty-three years. As appreciation for his life flowed, I experienced something otherworldly that Philippians 1:3 states:
"I thank my God every time I remember you." Thankfulness
became a haven where my emotions rested, albeit briefly.

When Mindy and I married in 1980, our hearts were
filled with dreams of a future that included a houseful of
little ones. We anticipated having our world turned on end
with the fullness of parenthood. We cherished the thought
of being a family. I had no doubt Mindy would make a
wonderful mom, and I could hardly wait to hear someone

call me Dad. Both of us were in the second half of our twenties, and we didn't want to wait long to begin that season of our lives.

However, our journey took considerably longer than we'd planned. Our struggle to conceive lasted five years and included a surgery and a surprise move that turned out to be an answer to prayer after our inital misgivings.

In the early days of our efforts, we assumed all would happen naturally. We didn't think much of it when a couple of months passed without getting pregnant. Over the next few months we took turns boosting each other's growing doubts with reminders that those things often take longer than expected; surely we still had no real reasons for worry.

After a couple of years had passed, our faith began to feel chipped by the chisel of waiting. We began to wonder if we would ever see our dream come true. We still told ourselves to trust God; surely he had a plan and it'd be a great one . . . right? We just had to keep trying and waiting. We consulted various doctors, who offered support but no real answers, and we held out some more.

During those years, as we researched the issues keeping us from pregnancy, doctors at the Mayo Clinic told us of a specialist in Dallas who was doing state-of-the-art infertility surgeries with excellent results. However, the logistics of distance between our home in Moline, Illinois, and Dallas, Texas, proved problematic at the time. Our jobs were a thousand miles from Dallas, and we felt our chances were slim to none of ever seeing our dream come true.

Eventually we felt bewildered and hopeless. We had begun to doubt our faith and even began blaming God.

We'd been open to adopting and had long since completed the paperwork with an agency through our church. The agency director, Krista, was a childhood friend and a fellow alumnus of the University of Illinois. Krista had been helping us for more than four years but to no avail. We were hopeful that the reason God might have postponed or even canceled our plans to have a biological child was because he had handpicked a little someone for us whom we might never meet if we'd already conceived. But each year when nothing came of it, our frustration multiplied.

And then things began to look up. A close family friend who was an ob-gyn told us about a teenage mother-to-be who, along with her parents' support, planned to give up the baby for adoption. The family wanted information on each of us. With mounting excitement, we faxed the requested documents.

Eventually we heard news that a healthy baby girl had been born and was waiting for us two hours away in a suburban Chicago hospital. Our lawyer FedExed the necessary papers, we bought a crib and quickly prepared a nursery, and our family and friends rejoiced with us.

We chose her name, Margaret Grafton Hallene, after eight generations of Margarets in our family. Grafton was Mindy's maiden name. We even contacted our minister to arrange a baptism date.

And then the day before we were to pick up Maggie, the

phone rang again. It was our doctor, who informed us that the biological mother had asked to see and hold her daughter. That type of request is not usually a positive sign for adoptive parents.

Mindy and I spent a sleepless night and got the inevitable call at eight o'clock the next morning. The mother had decided to keep the baby, the child we'd come to love as our own. Her parents were in full support of her decision.

And instead of getting into the car for the road trip of our lives, we gathered our broken hearts and unpacked the baby gear from the car: car seat, blankets, diapers, bottles of milk in a cooler.

After we shelved our dream once more, heartbreak turned to bitterness. We'd thought of that tiny girl as ours, so naturally we felt as though someone took our child from us. Our dream of having at least four kids, as we each had in our childhood families, seemed destined to remain unfulfilled.

Then in 1984, God worked the miracle that changed our home forever. I had been working for John Deere when I received the call about a position at Montgomery Elevator, the company my great-grandfather founded in 1892 and where my father had been president since 1968. The position was in the office in McKinney, Texas, a small town in the northern part of the state. We were hesitant about moving since we'd both grown up in the Quad Cities, and we were unsure of leaving behind our family, friends, and history. But move we did.

Somehow Mindy had kept the Dallas specialist's phone number, and shortly after we settled in Texas, she made an appointment with him. Four months of infertility drugs and shots preceded a five-hour operation in January 1985.

One month later, I was at work on the factory floor when my administrative assistant called me to say I had received a telegram marked urgent. As I raced to the office, a wave of fear engulfed me. Surely something must have happened to someone in our family. Who sent telegrams anymore, and urgent ones at that?

As I tore open the Western Union message, I saw that Mindy had sent it. *What gives?* I thought nervously. *Why didn't she just call me or drive the short distance to the factory to share what undoubtedly must have been bad news?*

Time stopped as I read her message: *WE DID IT!!! We are going to be parents in November!* No drug or drink could have been manufactured to create the euphoria I felt in the office that day. Thoughts of doctors' visits, sonogram pictures, and Lamaze classes flooded out the previous moments' fears.

Our baby was due toward the end of November 1985, near Thanksgiving, such a great time to welcome a child. We prepared a nursery again and filled it with gear and gifts from showers and shopping trips. We discussed names, adding to and crossing off our list as the calendar flipped through spring, summer, and halfway through fall.

The morning before Thanksgiving arrived, and we greeted it early—3:00 a.m. to be exact—with labor pains and a rushed trip to Dallas. After forty-five minutes of driving and an hour in the hospital, we knew Mindy had experienced a false alarm.

Then exactly twenty-four hours later on November 28, Thanksgiving Day, the labor pains returned in earnest. We drove back to the hospital, and this time it was no false alarm. After many hours of terrible back labor, Mindy finally felt it was time for Alex to make his debut.

I suppose our struggle wouldn't have been complete if she'd delivered easily. An emergency developed when Alex's heartbeat began dropping rapidly. The doctors wasted no time wheeling Mindy into surgery for a last-minute C-section, and Alex was born at last. But he was in grave danger because the umbilical cord had been wrapped around his neck.

I remember walking endlessly through the hospital halls. Time inched along as I willed the doctors to come through the doors with good news. I prayed to God, sometimes cursing him under my breath, saying, "First you make us wait five long years, and now you're going to take him away after only five hours with us."

But no. God let us keep baby Alex. The miracles continued when the doctors returned and announced that our son had struggled through his life-and-death ordeal. Both he and his tired but radiantly happy mother were going to be just fine.

Like Alex, I, too, had nearly died at birth, so from day one I felt a special bond with him as a fighter. I was so proud of him.

Eventually we brought our baby home and began to

settle in to our new lifestyle. My mother spent the first few days with us, and Mindy and I wondered what was so tough about having a newborn. We were sleeping great and feeling that parenthood was a breeze—until just after Mom boarded the plane back home to Moline. Ten days into caring for our baby, we understood lack of sleep and realized all that Mom had been doing for us.

We enjoyed introducing friends and family to our son. Mindy's mother had already passed away, but her dad visited soon after we arrived home. Pride lit his eyes, much as my own dad's face had glowed, as he counted each of Alex's fingers and toes and proclaimed him perfect.

Those first weeks were full as we thrilled over Alex's every sound, soaked up every snuggle, felt the effects of sleep deprivation, and loved it all. And so we were a family.

Before long we grew again, this time without as many challenges as we'd had getting started. Bryan William arrived seventeen months after Alex, and after another nineteen months, James Welsh completed our trilogy three years and one day after his oldest brother was born. When Alex visited Jimmy, hours old in the hospital, he pointed to him and said, "Baby." Then he pointed to Bryan and said, "Baby." And then he pointed to himself and proclaimed, "Big boy!"

My dad said I finally had my Irish triplets, Snip, Snap, and Snur, from books I'd read as a kid. He was right; my dream had come true.

Amid welcoming those bundles of joy, the company called again with a transfer back to Moline. We'd come to love our lives in Texas, but we saw the value of raising our children among our roots and relatives.

So we settled back home in western Illinois. And yes, we were busy. It wasn't just the number of children in our house; it was the pace they all kept. We had three rambunctious, all-boy boys. If Alex was the leader, then Bryan was quieter but ever so observant. He became an instigator, oftentimes in subtle ways. Jimmy is now more than six feet tall, and as a young child his mischievousness was just as big. They all poured their hearts and souls into whatever they did. And of course, being boys, they all created their share of stories that we still love to tell.

Alex was always a tough and gritty little guy. He was a fearless kid—full of zest for life with plenty of stitches and broken bones—who looked out for his little brothers.

His last day of second grade, when he broke both his arms falling from the monkey bars, he walked a mile home like a Viking, merely whimpering when he couldn't open the round front doorknob with his broken limbs. Thankfully, Mindy heard him, and I met them in the office of our pediatrician friend, Chris Moen. Dr. Chris then consulted another mutual friend and orthopedic surgeon and explained: "Al and Mindy's son, Alex, has a problem with his arms," his voice drawing out the unbelievable.

"Armzzz?" came the response, loud enough for us to overhear. Yes, both of them. Broken. One fall. Years later we still laugh over that when we all get together.

After the accident, when Alex's arms were encased in

blue Logan Leopards (his school's mascot) casts, my dad asked him how it happened.

"Well, Papa," Alex began philosophically, "I've made that second rung many times . . ." We think he must have been trying to show off to a little girl classmate, trying to prove his new third-grader mettle.

Though he wasn't a tall kid physically, Alex's heart was huge. A defender and a natural leader, he had a knack for noticing when others needed a friend and the compassion to be that friend. He never outgrew those skills.

And he didn't have a problem standing his ground when he felt wrong was done. I remember an incident when he was about four. When I arrived home from work, Mindy greeted me with, "Guess what your son did." I knew I was in for a doozy.

Apparently Alex had become incensed earlier in the day when his mother wouldn't let him play with his best friend Lars, Dr. Chris's son. Many children may have pouted, thrown a tantrum, stomped off, or refused to eat their veggies in retaliation.

Alex called 911.

Naturally Mindy was shocked when a squad car with blazing lights pulled up to our house. At first she thought I'd been killed on my way home from work. Adding embarrassment to the situation, two naked young Hallene boys raced past the officers and smacked right into the front door. Hey, if they couldn't run around natural in their own home, where else?

Laughing, one of the officers turned to Mindy. "Bath time?"

Despite the humor of the situation, they did their duty and examined each boy for bruises or evidence of abuse and were assured that our happy, healthy kids weren't being mistreated. Then they played up the incident by talking no-nonsense about the seriousness of calling 911.

I can only imagine the volume of Mindy's exasperation after they left, but I do remember that the boys were "my sons" once I got home that evening.

After we dealt with the situation at home, I took Mr. Alex Hallene down to the police station. A tall officer stood high and intimidating behind a large booking desk, and I instructed Alex to look up into his eyes, offer his hand, and apologize.

Alex shook his hand and said, "My brother made me do it." So much for my attempt at good parenting.

Though Mindy may not have laughed a great deal that day, she was a fabulous mother and still is. I've said many times over the years that there wasn't a better mom for boys. She was a tomboy who matched their energy and cheered for them in their different sports. A great athlete herself, she is the daughter of another hero of mine, Big Jim Grafton, who was a starter on Moline's second-place championship basketball team in 1943 and an Iowa Hawkeye basketball letterman, and who also served his country in the army air corps in World War II.

Mindy championed our sons, challenged them, loved on them, and built them up. She encouraged their hearts, accepted them for who they are, and inspired them to keep going for their dreams.

Speaking of dreams, one of the best things about raising sons has to be occupying the front-row seat to theirs. Their young playacting as valiant knights, mighty superheroes, ferocious bears, and fire-breathing dragons was not just fantasy to them at three, four, and five. They truly believed they were whatever characters they assumed, and I cherished the privilege of being caught up in their whirlwind as they tumbled through life.

We taught respect and discipline, and they were all good boys. But there's a reason why "boys will be boys" has become cliché; it carries a whopping nugget of truth.

One spring day while Mindy was out grocery shopping, a bad hailstorm from out of nowhere struck Moline. After seeing the hundreds of pings to our new Volvo, Mindy drove to our sister-in-law Molly's house to decompress over a cup of coffee. Alex and his cousin Benny went outside to inspect the vertical rows of indentations on our car in the driveway. After a while the doorbell rang, and Molly greeted an older woman who kindly asked, "Ma'am, do you want those little boys to make dents in the sides of your car?"

By then, Mindy had become familiar with her instinct that told her somewhere nearby a Hallene boy was into mischief. Sure enough, she and Molly found Alex and Benny with ball-peen hammers near our car. They had made more than two hundred horizontal "hail" dents in the sides of the car to match the vertical ones Mother Nature had made with real hail.

What was two hundred more among the countless others? At least they'd tried to be symmetrical with their work. Unfortunately, our insurance agent didn't laugh when he said they would cover only the vertical dents, as he doubted hail could cause such ninety-degree horizontal damage.

But Alex and Benny weren't done with their mischief. The next time, they set their sights on their grandfather's new white Cadillac. After a long rain, they put on their Teenage Mutant Ninja Turtle boots, then stomped through mud puddles and climbed all over the car—hood, roof, trunk—and jumped off to reload and go again. And people wondered why my hair had streaks of gray in my thirties.

But they did keep us laughing. When we visited my parents' church and my dad gave each boy a dime for the offering, Alex looked up at him dubiously and quipped, "We pay our teachers twenty-five cents at our church."

When he acted up during a trip to Florida at age ten, I gave him the choice of a spanking or push-ups. He chose the workout, and we started counting. True to his age, he had some adolescent attitude going on, so I added ten more each time he mouthed off. When he got to two hundred, he kept right on going but said, "How many more, Al?" He might as well have switched to only one arm and added some acrobatics for kicks. I burst out laughing, reached down to help him up, and probably said something parentally important. He could disarm anyone with charm, but he never got in real trouble and was loved by everyone.

Somewhere along the way he was dubbed "Yalex," a nickname that was coined because his name was first past our lips each time we needed to get the boys' collective attention. Calling "Alex" to no avail eventually became a holler that sounded like *Yalex*, and the rest is history.

Yalex was not alone in his shenanigans. His cohorts Bryan and Jimmy were always ready for adventure. Bryan, the quiet instigator, may have seemed a little milder, but Jimmy—oh my Jimmy. Mindy and I used to fall into bed each evening to get as much rest as possible before bracing ourselves to keep up with Jimbo in the morning.

Jimmy once drew with red magic marker all over our Dalmatian, Bonnie, to connect her dots, of course. He also put a box of Lucky Charms into a 350-degree oven to make hot cereal. We all found out cardboard catches fire at that temperature. He filled the toilet with golf balls. He stuck a lollipop in the barbershop hair dryer and claimed "I didn't do that" when the adults saw smoke billowing from the machine.

Once when he was a little older, he leaped over the tennis net to knock some honesty into a cheating competitor. His opponent had been calling balls in or out in favor of his own score. When Jimbo called him on it, the boy shot back a derogatory comment about Jimmy, who then hurdled the net and grabbed the kid before the adults intervened.

Actually, we were kind of proud of Jimmy for expecting such honesty, not to mention for clearing the net so easily. He was a sturdy kid.

I'm proud of my sons for being defenders when the situation called for it. Alex was the most consistent protector of his cousin Matt, but I recall one time when a couple of playground bullies pushed Matt down and stole his ball. A much younger Jimmy sped to the scene, punched both boys, and returned the ball to his cousin.

Our three "bruisers" earned their name. A couple of times they locked sitters in the closet, and they would run out the door as soon as Mindy and I arrived back home, saying as they fled, "Don't pay me. Don't call me." The little guys weren't hellions, but they could be a rowdy bunch.

So we made church a priority, as it had been for both of us growing up. We did our best to instill seeds of faith and to nurture Christian standards to help channel the testosterone. And I'm sure regular church attendance reminded Mindy and me to dole out healthy doses of grace and humor along with rules and discipline.

As the boys grew, our days filled with their activities. Aside from school, they all played several sports and sang for the Moline Boys Choir, which I had been part of in my younger years. Spring and early-summer Saturdays were all-day events at the baseball park. We'd pack a cooler and keep the schedule handy to steer each son to whichever field or double-header his team was playing. And, again, we loved it.

During those years, our home—affectionately dubbed our "Ponderosa"—was nestled toward the end of a quiet road near a tree-filled ravine where the boys loved to play with neighbor kids. There was plenty of room to explore among beautiful nature and out of the way of traffic. We even cleared a trail down through the ravine and up the other side to the next street for the kids to go back and forth to play.

We also tried to give the boys a sense of history. Each year we made a big deal about their birthdays and served them breakfast in bed on their special day. We traveled to Dallas to show them the maternity ward at Presbyterian Hospital where Alex and Bryan were born. We showed them our old home in McKinney and went to a Cowboys game, Bryan's favorite, even though his brothers always favored our Chicago Bears. We made yearly visits to my folks' condo in Naples, Florida, as well as trips to the lake in Minnesota and to another lake in Wisconsin, where Mindy's family owned a cabin.

Tradition and generations played a significant role in their growing-up years and still do in their adult years. Alex and his best friend, Lars, followed in Chris's and my footsteps on Logan's Student Congress, just as Chris and I had followed our fathers' footsteps on the Moline School Board. Chris and I treated our sons to an annual skip day from school to ride roller coasters at Six Flags Great America near Chicago. Some memories are worth breaking a rule or two.

We loved the connections we made. Our friends had friends who also became our friends and vice versa, and our neighbors joined us for a Christmas celebration on December 23 each year. We got involved with one another, and we tried to teach by example the value of approaching life and relationships wholeheartedly.

Obviously, the Quad Cities area has offered belonging and identity to our family. Mindy and I were thankful to raise our kids in middle-class America. In many ways we were living the American dream. My friend Jim, who helped me the morning of Alex's death, once said, "If ever there was a typical American family, the Hallenes were it." One marriage, three kids, and Bonnie the dog. A nice home, productive jobs, and influential roles serving the community. We had it good. We still do, but like everyone else's, our story has weathered some bumps and bruises along the way.

We remained busy into our sons' teen years, and I've wondered if perhaps I stayed too busy with work and community involvements, such as serving as chairman of Junior Achievement and on the time-consuming school board, eventually as president. Somewhere along the way our marriage hit rocky waters, and our daily home life changed.

Mindy and I divorced in 2000, when the boys were fifteen, thirteen, and twelve. I moved to a Cape Cod–style house in a 1950s Beaver Cleaver neighborhood, three doors down from where my Hallene grandparents lived. My mother still lives six blocks away from me, in the house I grew up in. If the geography is confusing, just think "comfort returning to my roots" and "welcomed connections." As a kid, I played in my current house with one of my kindergarten friends, and the same trees that lined the street several decades ago still shelter the neighborhood today. Home is a big deal, and Mindy and I did our best to ensure that the boys still had a sense of home in both houses.

As we all tried to adjust to the divorce, my nearby home made it possible for ongoing and frequent visits with Alex, Bryan, and Jimmy. I had been traveling all over the country for work, plus going back and forth to teach at the University of Iowa in Iowa City. I needed to see the boys, so I cut the travel and focused on teaching, which I love.

As more years cycled, Alex collected roles, and he excelled at everything he did. He was son, big brother, grandson, cousin, friend to all—a host, if you will—a multi-talented athlete, a street-smart nice kid, and a leader. He was co-captain of his high school tennis team, senior-class vice president at MHS, co-chair of homecoming that year, named Superfan because of his school spirit, and a member of the all-conference academic team. He was very outgoing and went to his share of school dances, dated some, and enjoyed a full social life.

In many ways Alex was a typical teen, but he also stood out. He had a quality about him that drew others in, a natural success in many ways. And he was funny and could be a prankster.

He and Lars paired up once for a doughnut-eating fundraiser to help hungry children. He was the manager, and Lars did the eating. They did well, and when the Christmas season arrived soon after, they sent out a photo card to their sponsors, thanking them for the support and inviting them to help out again the next year. How many seventeen-year-old guys would do that?

Although all my boys played several sports, in time each one discovered his favorite. I can't pass up a proud-dad moment to say that all three made it to state: Alex in tennis; Bryan in tennis and almost in golf; and Jimmy as starting linebacker for Moline, twice making it to the state playoffs. I collected newspaper stories that featured my kids and highlighted their interview quotes to show the grand-kids someday.

But what impressed me most was when I'd see a giving nature reveal itself in their activities. I'd learned from ear-lier generations that community service and looking out for others need to be high priorities, or the other accolades don't matter so much. Service makes a lasting impact.

Ever since he was small, Alex's heart for others shone in a special way. He looked out for people. He included his brothers and their friends with a hand of welcome instead of superiority.

In Alex's condo on October 2, 2008, I basked in the memories for those brief moments as I thought about our history together. I recalled the joy of finally becoming a father. I looked down at my grown son who was gone from this earth and remembered how his mother and I had spent months anticipating his arrival and all the years since then.

Then, as with the other messages, I felt the gift fading beneath the tragedy that was returning to engulf me once more. These fond memories withdrew, and it was just Alex and me again in October 2008. I held on to gratitude as long as I could, kissed my son, and thanked him for fighting so hard to live on the day he was born so that he could pave the way for his two younger brothers. I thanked him for being the leader of our little pack, who all his life had led his brothers with a solid heart. I also thanked him for doing so well as the oldest and firstborn in our family, not often an easy role to fulfill. I was the oldest, too, so I knew something about the responsibility carried by an oldest son. I knew Alex had done a far better job of that than I had done.

As this album of remembrance faded, I thanked God, who I knew was there with us, for allowing me the honor and joy of being Alex's earthly father.

Chapter Five

Matters of Life

AL, MINDY, AND ALEX, BAPTISM DAY, FIRST UNITED
METHODIST CHURCH, MCKINNEY, TEXAS, SPRING 1986

PAPA AND ALEX, NAPLES BEACH, GULF OF MEXICO, SPRING 1986

ALEX (AGE 3) AND
AL, LAKE MAY,
WALKER, MINNESOTA,
SUMMER 1989

THE HALLENE FAMILY, MOLINE, ILLINOIS, CHRISTMAS 1990

THE HALLENE BOYS, CHRISTMAS CARD PICTURE, CHRISTMAS 1991

LOGAN ELEMENTARY
DAD'S CLUB BASEBALL
K–2, COACH AL WITH
JIMMY, BRYAN, AND
ALEX WITH TWO
BROKEN ARMS,
SUMMER 1993

JIMMY (AGE 5), BRYAN (AGE 7), AND ALEX (AGE 8), ON THE HALLENE DOCK, LAKE MAY, SUMMER 1994

ALEX (AGE 8), BATTING PRACTICE, LOGAN ELEMENTARY DAD'S CLUB BASEBALL, SUMMER 1994

ALEX, HIS BROTHERS, AND MATT ON BIKES IN MIMI
AND PAPA'S NEIGHBORHOOD, SUMMER 1994

THE HALLENE FAMILY, CHRISTMAS 1994

ALEX WITH
BRACES (AGE 13)

PAPA AND ALEX, LAKE MAY, SUMMER 2000

PAPA AND MIMI'S 50TH ANNIVERSARY, SMUGGLERS'
INN RESORT, VERMONT, JUNE 2001

ALEX, TENNIS COCAPTAIN,
MOLINE HIGH SCHOOL
TENNIS COURTS,
SPRING 2003

BRYAN (AGE 18), JIMMY (AGE 17), AL, ALEX (AGE 20) HALLENE
FAMILY CHRISTMAS CARD, MOLINE, ILLINOIS, 2005

ALEX (AGE 21), CASTING WITH JIMMY (AGE 18) IN ALEX'S RED
BOAT, LAKE MAY, WALKER, MINNESOTA, SUMMER 2007

ALEX (AGE 3), SUNSET, NAPLES BEACH, GULF OF MEXICO, WINTER 1988

Even though I walk through the valley of the
shadow of death, I will fear no evil, for you are with
me; your rod and your staff, they comfort me.

PSALM 23:4 (ESV)

I'm not sure how many times I've seen the 2000 movie *Gladiator*, but it has become classic to me. Set amid the sweeping rule of the Roman Empire, the film is brutal and raw, and it is beautiful. It zeros in on the story of one man, the great Maximus Decimus Meridius: husband, father, warrior, and the emperor's chosen man to return the empire to a republic.

And then he lost it all. His wife and son were savagely murdered in an act of jealousy. Stripped of his position, Maximus found himself lowered to the existence of a slave, a gladiator forced to fight in the arena. His unspeakable losses resonate with me, as does his grip on hope of a future reunion to get him through sorrow.

One day in the slave quarters where the gladiators trained, Maximus and his friend Juba talked about seeing their loved ones after they died. Juba said he would wait for his family in the afterlife because most certainly he would get there before them.

Maximus: "My wife and my son are already waiting for me."

Juba: "You will meet them again. But not yet. Not yet."[1]

Not yet. Not yet. These words have become a battle cry of sorts for me, a reminder not of the hope of fictional characters, but of the promises of God.

I still know that God showed up for me in the condo. No, he had already been there with Alex. The God who met me the morning of Alex's death would never have left my son alone in his suffering the previous night. God simply stayed for me.

The mind can conjure up terrible images when left to roam. I'm thankful that God collected my thoughts when I couldn't after finding Alex. He communicated to me perfectly in those moments and gave me clarity through the fog of grief, which assured me these messages were from him. These experiences will hold me through this life into eternity.

But God wasn't done that day in Champaign. He had a few resolutions ready for my questions and some things to tell me about this earthly existence. At the heart of my questions was the big one: *Why?* Seeing Alex lifeless made no sense. I had only seen him alive, had never imagined that scene hitting my eyes and implanting itself in my head. Also, *why* did all my efforts to meet his needs not make the life-saving difference for him?

God began to respond to my questions that day, but even so, the questions still can seem never ending and prompt me to second-guess every minute decision. Did we take him to the right counselors? Should we have encouraged him to take a semester off or transfer to a college closer to us, such as Augustana in nearby Rock Island, where Bryan and Jimmy both went? Was there any clue we should have caught or any other way we could have intervened? We learned soon after his death that he had lunch plans with a friend the next day and plans to travel to an away game that weekend. So why end it all that night? So much left to wonder about; the whys and if onlys are enough to drive a person mad.

Another question that has plagued me is whether Alex could have been saved if I'd had the lucidity to call my friend Jim at six o'clock that morning to check on him instead of driving all the way down there to do it myself. That likely would have still been too late, but if I'd charged my phone in my bedroom instead of in the living room, would I have heard it ring? Did Alex's life hang on an arbitrary decision like so many others we all make every day?

We're given one lifetime on this earth, and much of it is loaded with whys. So much is beyond our control. How many of our moments—and ultimately our survival—are subject to the whims of random occurrence, or to evil, or to our own brokenness?

I suppose all those questions can be summed up with two: Is God loving and powerful enough to care for us, and how can any of us be sure we aren't missing something vital that would make all the difference?

Welcome message number four.

God confirmed to me that he is involved in the details of our lives, undeniably and intimately. Each minute, month, year, and decade. Amen to that any day of the week, but especially on one that serves up circumstances we can't make sense of on our own.

In this fourth gift, God impressed on my heart Matthew 6:25, Jesus' words from two thousand years ago: "Therefore I tell you, do not worry about your life, what you will eat or drink; or about your body, what you will wear. Is not life more than food, and the body more than clothes?"

Jesus went on to compare us to the birds of the air that don't sow or reap or store away in barns, but who instinctively rely on our heavenly Father to provide for them. And aren't we more valuable? Worry can't add anything to life (vv. 26–27). Then Jesus spoke about the lilies growing in the field. They don't labor or spin, yet not even King Solomon in all his splendor was dressed like them (vv. 28–29).

And then he summed up the crux of those examples: "Seek first his kingdom and his righteousness, and all these things will be given to you as well. Therefore, do not worry about tomorrow, for tomorrow will worry about itself. Each day has enough trouble of its own" (vv. 33–34).

The chill returned, and I finally understood that passage from the Bible. Tears flowed again as I combed Alex's hair with my fingers and closed his eyes for the last time. I marveled at the well-formed body of my son as if it were the first time I had ever seen him. When along the way had I lost focus on the miracle of life? At that moment, the wonder came back. Alex's man-sized fingers and hands were just as miraculous as they'd been nearly twenty-three years earlier. I saw in my full-grown child the same deep vulnerability that prompted me to protect him fiercely when he was a newborn.

I recalled my first moments with him, how I'd watched his tiny chest heave as he gasped for breath. After he was out of the woods, I remembered touching each little finger and toe and waiting for his squinty eyes to open so I could connect with him. He looked around as if to say, *Where am I? I wanna go back!* And everything in me moved to make him as comforted and secure as he'd been in the womb.

But now instead of hearing his breath, I heard my own labored breathing. How easily we forget the miracle.

I had overlooked the importance of Jesus' words through the years in my selfish worries about bills, houses, cars, jobs—things that finally became irrelevant, or for that matter, never mattered most.

I understood in a more complete way that we came into life with nothing other than a body and a soul. I recalled God's recent gift of memories from Alex's life. The order of the messages still amazes me. They came in perfect order and precision, as God meant them to build on one another. I'd just been remembering Alex as a pure, needy newborn, then throughout his growing years. All those reminders led to this fourth message that impressed on my heart the value of human life.

I wonder about the pressures Alex carried to measure up to some worldly standard of acceptability, a perceived need to prove himself to the breaking point. I do think school stress played into Alex's depression, and I wonder how much worry he battled to achieve the levels of success set by others. The enemy can twist truth and cause the strongest of us to lose focus on what really matters; we question our worth, and our hope is suffocated. I can understand some of these pressures because I faced similar ones as a young man and actually throughout my life.

My father was my hero. Alan Montgomery Hallene Sr. was a man with a giant presence who excelled at everything he did. He grew up a farm boy in Orion, Illinois, and he claimed that the University of Illinois made his life. Because Illinois was a land-grant university at the time, he and my mother could attend for fifty dollars a semester. They both made good on that investment.

They met on the Quad there, as he was making a name for himself academically. He is listed on the school's prestigious Bronze Tablet for graduating in the top 3 percent of the class of 1951, an incredible achievement at such a pressure-cooker institution. He was salutatorian of his class of roughly five thousand, and his picture hangs in the Illini Union for being president of the Alumni Association and the University of Illinois Foundation (the university's fundraising arm). In 1985 he accepted the highest lifetime achievement award because of his volunteerism.

After he graduated, he didn't plan to work at Montgomery

Elevator. But after a death in the family, he left his job at the Atomic Energy Commission in 1953 to keep Montgomery within the family. He served as president there from 1968 until he retired in 1994. During his years of leadership, the business thrived to become the largest privately held company in the elevator industry, ranked fourth in total elevator and escalator sales and first in escalators. The company even took Neil Armstrong the first ninety feet to the moon, to get him to the top of the Apollo spacecraft! In 1994 the company was sold to KONE Corporation, marking the end of an era.

Alex was about nine years old the first time he asked me about the decision to sell Montgomery. "I wanted to be president there someday, Dad." My heart caught in my throat. I was feeling miserable myself about the whole change, but I was moved by his pride in our family history. It showed his maturity at a young age and contrasted with the embarrassment I'd felt most of my life surrounded by the aura of my dad's success.

At seven or eight, Alex asked me why we didn't name him Alan III. He could have blown me over with a feather. All my early life I detested being called Junior. In fact, I grew up as Lanny until my older grade-school years. Some family and long-time friends still call me Lan, and I love it as an endearing term. But Junior was terrible to me.

I was in my thirties when I finally began to enjoy my dad's greatness instead of wanting to run from it. I recognized the opportunity to work with him at Montgomery, where I could glean from his brilliance and superb people skills.

Then to see my young son feeling proud that his middle name was Montgomery and saying he would have loved to be the fifth generation of our family to work there, I didn't have an adequate answer for him. The real answer was we had gotten too big and profitable for a smallish company to compete internationally with the biggest players in the industry.

I've thought that Alex might be alive today if we still had the company. Had we known of Alex's senior-year academic difficulties, if he had been more comfortable telling us, he could have taken a break as many college students do and worked in the factory until he could regain his footing. We'll never know.

Alex had a lot to look up to on Mindy's side of the family as well. Her father, whom my boys called Papa Jim, was an amazing man. He was the owner of Blackhawk Foundry in Davenport, Iowa, and he served on the Moline Park Board as president from 1969 to 1977.

As for my parents, they've always given back to their alma mater, and in 1998 they were honored for their generosity when the Hallene Gateway at the university's east entrance was erected and named after them. A carving at the top reads *Learning & Labor*, and it's an impressive piece of architecture. The arch was originally a portal entrance from a university building that had been torn down. In the years since its repurpose, the Gateway has welcomed every student who joins the orange and blue ranks of the Fighting

Illini. Our extended family was on hand at the dedication, and the pictures reveal the pride we felt in the legacy our parents had built.

I followed in their footsteps by studying there, as did my brother. Although I did fine, I had to work my tail off for every grade. I continually carried a burden to prove myself, always unsure if I could measure up to the bar my father had set so high. I enjoy mentioning that I was proficient in freshman rhetoric, the one course he earned a B in during his college career. My dad spoke at my graduation in 1974 in the 17,000-seat assembly hall.

In his later years he served on the board of the MacArthur Foundation, a role that connected him with a renowned peer group that included radio broadcaster Paul Harvey, polio-vaccine developer Jonas Salk, Treasury Secretary William Simon, US Attorney General Edward Levi, and Nobel Prize–winner Murray Gell-Mann.

Being his son was an honor, albeit an intimidating one. Yet he never lorded his successes over me—quite the contrary. He encouraged me to reach for my own potential and used his experience, skills, and giant heart to build me up. He and Mom raised us with Luke 12:48 in mind: "From everyone who has been given much, much will be required" (NASB). And he was once quoted as saying, "Life is people, and I love people. How you relate to them is what life is all about."

Despite the academic pressures, much of our family legacy began at Illinois, because if my old man hadn't run into Mom on the Quad in 1947, we wouldn't exist! In fact, as a way to give back, I have dreams to create a foundation that would offer free campus-based Christian counseling for students and veterans. Perhaps others could be helped as they deal with school, career, and other stressors.

Based on conversations Alex initiated with me over the years, I know he loved U of I and our family legacy both there and at home in Moline.

Still, I do think he carried some burden to make proud the generations ahead of him. He called me his hero and occasionally listed off my responsibilities and civic service. "How did you do it, Dad? You're my hero. You got a mechanical engineering degree from a top-flight school and then a PhD from Iowa. You were successful at John Deere, plant manager at Montgomery, Moline school board president . . ."

Each time, his questions revealed something of his ambitions and possibly some self-doubt about whether he could be successful. Each time I'd say, "You'll do those things too, Alex. Look at all you've done already in your young life." I'd explain that I always felt street-smart but academically dumb compared to my all-wise, Paul Newman–blue-eyed father. I felt destined to be a B player in the business world. Then at John Deere I learned that if I worked a little harder and longer and was nice to people—very easy things for me and for Alex—the promotions would come.

As we talked, I'd list his achievements in sports and student government and his character qualities that I'd always been fully confident would take him far in life. He'd always been tenacious, a high achiever who may have been his own toughest critic. I really thought we had good conversations about it all. But those ambitions seem like rubbish now in comparison to the life of my son.

Alex was majoring in finance like my younger brother, Jim (Uncle Chip to my boys). Alex was looking forward to beginning work with Jim after his supposed December 2008 graduation. He was in his fifth year of college that fall, and it looked as though he would be further delayed in graduating. I believe this delay is the reason Alex took his life.

Somewhere along the way, though he never would tell us, he either dropped out or didn't enroll that semester. Because of his age, we couldn't legally find out without his written permission. We chose not to delve into this out of respect for him. Whatever the case, he was not going to make the December 2008 time frame, and I believe hopelessness took over. He felt stuck, caught in the system, and he was so conscientious and didn't want to shame the family.

Alex grew up loving the University of Illinois, everything about it, and may have felt he wasn't living up to his dream. He excelled at tennis in high school, but when the time came to apply to colleges and I asked him if he'd want to go to a smaller school where he could really enjoy playing the sport, he said, "Dad, I want to go to Illinois. I've dreamed of going there since I was five." He began his application essay with those words.

But every day on the way to campus that final semester, he drove past the Gateway, an ever-present reminder of the Hallene high bar. I will never recover from unwittingly contributing to the pressure by taking him and his brothers all those years to Illini games with their school friends.

Alex left this life with only his soul. Everything he'd experienced, accomplished, failed at, feared, dreamed of, and owned did not go with him into eternity. We leave this life with nothing more than what's been instilled in our souls on earth, yet we often fail to pay the most attention to what's beyond the here and now. On the day of Alex's death, God awakened me to his greater way, and I approach life differently as a result. I view life and people through God's corrective lens.

I know how much I love my sons and always will. At times I have felt bad for friends who couldn't have kids. I am grateful I had Alex for twenty-two years. I'd even have welcomed twenty-two months, twenty-two weeks, twenty-two days, or even twenty-two seconds rather than not at all. I would do anything I could to care for my kids; but being human, I could get sidetracked by everyday pressures.

Yet is anything on this earth more important than caring for people, body and soul? Since the Creator watches over and provides for his nature that he himself formed, he will prioritize us, his masterpieces created in his image (Gen. 1:27). He knows us to our cores. When I consider the stunning beauty of Genesis, the intimate way God gave human beings life, I am stilled. The one who knows our most naked, broken places is always on hand to meet us as we are.

When I felt consumed by guilt and inadequate as a father to save my son, God stopped my blame game by refocusing me on the celebration of Alex's life. Again, it's God's grace that he would show me his love through this tragedy. Through these four messages so far—the view of my dad and son alive and together, the promise that God knew the number of Alex's days, gratitude for being Alex's father, and this one about the value of life—he was leading me to see his big picture, which guided me through the pain.

I thought again of my family, how God had led me to my children's beautiful mother and allowed us to marry. How he had given us three incredible sons and a host of relatives and friends to celebrate life with. And how he was giving me this staying power in the wake of our loss, the knowledge and even a picture that Alex was happy, healthy, and more whole than earth allows.

The Lord showed me that he is about life, and not just life as we experience it in our seventy or eighty—or twenty-two—years, but life beyond what we can imagine.

I don't know that I could have grasped these concepts more fully than through the tactile experience of holding one most precious to me after his earthly time ended. I knew then that there is no point wasting these years on unimport-ant ventures that don't point toward our life Source.

Even though a lot of spiritual things have happened to me, those moments with God and Alex after Alex's death were set apart. They moved me beyond how I'd ever under-stood the Lord speaking to me. Maybe the intensity of the parent-child bond took me to a different level of grief;

perhaps my added life experiences had primed me to be ready for more understanding.

Whatever the case, God showed me that he is very close in death, as he is present and active in life. Unfortunately it's easy to miss him in the push of earning a living, dealing with the tyrannies of the urgent, and planning for college, retirement, and next year's vacation. It's easy to miss our loved ones around us, too, whom we can see and touch.

Being human, I surely missed some of what's most important as I sprinted and sometimes slogged through years of the daily grind. But while I sat with Alex, God planted a new purpose in me not to wallow but to move forward focused on his priorities, to help others discover the life he offers. He was able to do this in the midst of an earthly death because his presence and purpose transcend everything—death, heartache, pain, guilt, regret, remorse—to meet a soul in need of him.

Alex met the Source of life in person on October 2, 2008. Any doubts I might have had regarding Jesus' place in his life were laid to rest by the Lord himself when he later met me.

I am learning that God provides certain anchors for our faith, and I'm still holding on to the ones he gave me in those ten short minutes. These anchors testify to his faithfulness and promises, but we have to choose to keep living by faith. That choice can be very difficult to make when life delivers a blow.

When my memory battles questions, I have to release them to God in order to hang on to my faith, not to mention my sanity. He reminds me that he was there caring for me, just as he was present with Alex. He already told me that he knew the number of Alex's days, and the day of Alex's death was not happenstance. The Lord was there, keeping all in hand.

We are not granted a pass from pain on earth. Healing may not come here. But we are guaranteed a perfect forever, complete healing, unending peace, incomparable joy, and an eternal adventure if we don't miss the Source who makes the difference. Because of him, we can live free from worry, as Alex does now.

When images too heavy to bear and thoughts of Alex's broken heart berate my mind, I have to put those burdens back on God and accept instead the thoughts I can bear. To be honest, the choice is a constant battle. But I am buoyed by visions of Alex alive and well with the Lord, Alex in no more pain, and Alex completely healed and whole. He is peaceful. He is secure. He would not want to return to earth. I have always wanted the best for my children, and I can rest without worry about Alex because I know he is experiencing the best.

As I've processed this message, I've wondered what bodies Matthew 6:25 might refer to other than our physical ones. Perhaps the body of my family or my friends in need, possibly my country, or even my brothers and sisters in the body of Christ, as 1 Corinthians 12:12 refers to. I'm still figuring this out, but God is giving me time to discover it. I do know that I owe it to Alex not to miss what matters most for the rest of my days. Perhaps God will use me and my experience to help someone else. I pray it may be so.

Chapter Six

God Is a Dad Too

He does not ignore those in trouble.
He doesn't hide from them
but listens when they call out to him.
PSALM 22:24 (NCV)

As the previous sensing faded, reality returned and my body began to tremble from the emotional takeover. I may as well have been split open; never had I felt so undone. *Beyond* is an appropriate word to describe it all. Beyond bearing, beyond understanding, beyond how I'd thought I could hurt.

I wanted more time with Alex; I wasn't ready to let him go. I still had dreams for him. He had dreams for himself. He hadn't completed graduation, yet I had been primed to burst with pride as I watched his future develop after college.

I wouldn't see all three of my sons continue relationships with one another as they aged, wouldn't get to welcome the love of his life into our family or be father of the groom at his wedding. Whom and when would he have married? He'd never experience fatherhood. I'd never hold grandchildren from him, never say of his firstborn as my own father had said of mine that when your child has a child, life goes on. I wasn't sure whether I'd explode or implode from the crushing of those dreams.

I clutched Alex tightly. Maybe if I could merge us physically I wouldn't lose this person who was such a part of me. I'm convinced the parent-child bond can't be severed without a tearing of spirits, inner bloodshed. Anger at the injustice flared again. The idea of letting go was maddening. I was no more ready to release my son at twenty-two years than I'd been when he'd fought for life his first five hours. God had given him back to us then. If only one more time—it would be so easy for him to repeat the miracle. But I knew that miracle was not coming this time.

Alex had been too little to comprehend our celebration when he was born, and he wasn't there to see how impossible it was for me to say good-bye when he died. I had never agreed to say good-bye to him, especially not this way and not before my own time. I thought I should have been consulted about this major event in my son's life.

The way my thoughts tumbled, I'm sure mere seconds passed before another message snapped me out of them. This fifth one was so strong I felt as if God himself whispered the words into my ear. Although I have yet to hear his voice physically, my spirit heard clearly.

I feel your pain, Al, for I also lost my Son.

Thousands of Sunday school lessons, church sermons, Easter celebrations, Bible study meetings, funerals, prayers, and so on did not bring the clarity of that one spoken sentence from him.

My body stilled. Peace hovered and descended as the splayed shreds of my spirit drew back together in the Almighty's presence, and a new revelation began to form.

He was offering me the comfort of our mutual connection as fathers. I had always been skeptical that he had truly lost his Son. He knew he was going to raise him after only three days in the grave, whereas I could not bring Alex back. But through this vision, I realized God had actually loved a Son. And then after his Son's brief but meaningful life, he lost him cruelly and experienced a broken heart because of that loss.

I was affected, but I still wasn't clear how to process God's sharing the depths of his heart with me. I'd always envisioned him as distant and aloof; it was Jesus who had come close and touched us here on earth.

This message awakened me to what God must have gone through, not from the standpoint of church history or a Bible lesson, but as an emotionally invested Father. I had never grasped that God felt the tragic loss of his child—after all, he was in charge of everything and could have prevented Jesus' death.

True, Jesus had known what his purpose was on earth. John 6:38 shows that he was surrendered to his Father's plan: "For I have come down from heaven to do the will of God who sent me, not to do my own will" (NLT). He even talked of his upcoming death, showing that he was on board with that plan (Matt. 16:21).

However, Jesus' knowledge and godhood did not dilute the pain of death and separation from his Father. At his most human on the cross, the Son cried out, in essence, "Dad, where did you go? Why have you left me?" (Matt. 27:46, paraphrased).

I'd always viewed this verse from Jesus' perspective because the text doesn't give much detail from his Father's point of view. Although I knew that God couldn't coexist with the evil that Jesus carried for us on the cross (Hab. 1:13), I still can't envision turning my back on my child. Ever.

But God's holiness that rejected the sin Jesus bore did not dull the Father's pain. In fact, having to forsake his Son would have compounded his own agony. In order to save us, God had to make the excruciating choice to stand down instead of rescuing his child. He had to allow the trials, the dehumanizing acts of the thorns and spitting and cursing, the freeing of a known thief in his Son's place, the scourgings and beatings, the pounding of the spikes, and the hours of slow suffocation until death.

As a fellow father, I cannot fathom following through as he did. If I had been with Alex his final night on earth, nothing could have made me stand down and watch him be overtaken. I saw with new insight the depth of their Father-Son bond.

I can recall memories beyond number from the two-plus

decades Alex and I shared. But as powerful as my bonds are with my sons, I know they still don't carry the magnitude of the relationship between God and his Son, an ancient and holy history, sacred and void of human limitation. Their connection went far beyond human ties.

I suddenly knew that a God-sized heart throbs with God-sized pain. No matter that his Son understood the plan, the Father's heart must have broken.

When Christ hung battered on the cross, I wonder if God the Father recalled their closeness from before creation, the unity they'd shared even before sin arrived to destroy humanity. That sin was the first death, the one that set in motion our need for God to sacrifice his Son. They'd always known it would happen.

But when the day of the cross came, I wonder what thoughts filled the Father's mind. Perhaps he recalled his boy as a tiny newborn in the Bethlehem stable, or Jesus' toddler fist holding a carpenter's hammer, or twelve-year-old Jesus commanding a temple audience. I wonder at his thoughts as Jesus walked the long path to Golgotha, as his Firstborn over creation stumbled beneath the timber's load.

Did he look on Jesus' mother and wonder how she would survive such a loss? Did he long to draw Jesus' brothers close to steady them?

And through it all, who comforted God? Did the remaining two members of the holy Trinity offer solace to each other? Did the Spirit minister to the Father by saying, *Remember, we're not finished yet*? Surely no reminder was needed. But even the knowledge that he would bring Jesus back to life on the third day didn't negate the torment.

Who's to say the darkness and thunder at Jesus' death wasn't God's sorrow resounding over the universe, the rending of the temple curtain the severing of his heart? He had provided us freedom from death, but at the ultimate cost to his own Son and to himself.

If I ever were to doubt God's heart as a Father, I can look further back in Scripture to see how he felt about his boy. At Jesus' baptism by John the Baptist, the Father opened the heavens, and Jesus "saw the Spirit of God descending like a dove and settling on him. And a voice from heaven said, 'This is my dearly loved Son, who brings me great joy'" (Matt. 3:16–17 NLT). That's the voice of a proud Papa communicating his feelings to his Son.

God had been so filled with love and pride that he spoke for all to hear and rained down peace over his child. He let Jesus know he was there for him, and the Son could be assured of his Dad's blessing. Any child hearing his father talk publicly about him or her on that level would remember the experience forever.

The Bible's recordings of God speaking audibly are few and far between—most occurring in the times of the Old Testament hundreds of years before the cross—all reserved for his most important messages. As his Son was preparing to launch his ministry and fulfill his purpose on earth, his

Father had overflowed with delight. How well I know those paternal emotions.

Then came Jesus' death and their once-in-eternity separation. We can't comprehend all it cost them.

And then, two thousand years later on an unexpected day in my life, that God of eternity came to me, Father to father, and showered the same peace over me. In my greatest devastation, God spoke his comfort as close to audibly as it could have been. He knew the import of these moments in my life and in my own family's history—this event so altering that it would mark a line between all that had come before and everything yet to be.

He felt the pain of my son's death just as he had felt the grief of his own Son's, and he felt my heartache too. Even though Alex had known I loved him, I couldn't be there at his darkest hour. Our heavenly Father understood what I was enduring more than anyone else could. He had to choose to stand down. Unfathomable.

This message was the smoking gun for me. After going to church every Sunday for fifty-six years and hearing the crucifixion story a million times, I finally got it.

At that moment, God the Father was humbly saying to me, *I know, Al. It hurts so very badly.* Along with the holy hush of his majesty, I felt his friendship, a kinship as fathers I'd never experienced. I felt his kindness, too, and was impressed with the truth that God is too nice a guy not to make a way for us to reunite with those we've loved on earth. That may sound as if I'm humanizing almighty God, but he drew near to identify with my feelings that he had created in the image of his own. He made his heart human so I could understand him more, as his child and as a father.

The father-son legacy is vital to our wholeness as men, and I suppose it can be something our egos feel weighted by as well. My relationship with my own dad had been solid. But as men, we dread the idea of not leaving a worthwhile mark, of being lesser men than our forebears.

Alex would have been the fourth generation to graduate from Illinois. If my guess is correct, a further delay of graduation and its impact on his upcoming job with his uncle may have seemed like a failure to him. Living encumbered by the atmosphere of success throughout a campus like the University of Illinois can crush the spirit of the most driven student. When striving takes such center stage, balanced living and spiritual focus often pay a high cost.

Maybe Alex's depression hit hard when his questions about his future were running at an all-time high, and everything seemed to cave in for him.

My heart hurts to think of it all.

This message from God the Father let me know that we are constantly in his heart as well, as Jesus was that long-ago day. Although the Father could not look at his Son on the cross, his own heart was not unaffected by his child's torture. As he held back his power to spare Jesus so he could share eternal life with my sons and me, Jesus was still all over his heart.

To assume it did not hurt him beyond any human wound would be to disrespect the enormity of his loss. He did not shield himself from the horrors of the spiritual world known only to him, and the evils of hell he bars from our sight. Even though people face unspeakable injustices on earth, he protects us from vastly more. Yet his Son and his own almighty heart were unprotected from the enemy. Granted, hell's fury did not threaten him, but his Son endured evil's fullness.

God the Father hurt. Though I can't imagine a greater pain than mine at Alex's death, God hurt even beyond our heartaches, because his heart is profoundly greater than ours. That was his reality that terrible day.

As God ordered my thoughts, I still would have given my right arm to see Alex wake up. I would have traded places with him in an instant. I'm not sure when I stopped begging for that while I willed the police to delay their arrival.

I have to live with the dissonance created from attempting to meld the contrary emotions of knowing Alex is out of pain, yet feeling cheated out of spending decades with him.

Part of me, of course, still wants to have Alex back. Time has not diminished the longing even a little. But he's better where he is. I never would want him to leave earth the way he did, but now he is with God his Father, and it would not be better for him to return here.

I can't see it all with God's vision, but I have to trust his heart as a Father and rest in his comfort. I can't hold Alex anymore on earth, but I am comforted beyond this life.

When pain consumed me, the Father braced me with the truth that he holds Alex closer than ever.

I still wonder how I could have understood any of this so clearly at the time. It had to have been God. This sensing didn't cure me of grief, but it has given me a new and permanent picture of God our Father, who is also our benevolent friend. He reminded me that others still needed me on earth. I was still responsible for my other two sons and my mom, and I had to keep going.

I don't remember whether my grip on Alex eased at that point, but I know that our Father's did not. I trust he will continue to see my sorrow Father to father. I trust he says, *I've got our boy. He's here with mine. All is well and you'll meet again.* And despite the ache, I thank him for speaking truth.

Chapter Seven

On the Bridge to the Other Side

I lift my eyes to you, O God, enthroned in heaven.
We keep looking to the LORD our
God for his mercy . . .
PSALM 123:1–2 (NLT)

When Alex was three, he was the ring bearer in his godfather, Uncle Chip's, wedding. He took his job as seriously as a preschooler can.

The venue was the elegant Broadmoor resort in Colorado Springs. Everyone was dressed to the nines, and Alex looked small, dark, and so handsome in his tux. The wedding party assembled at the top of a grand mahogany stairway that curved down to the main floor where the ceremony would take place. When the first chords of the organ rang with the processional, little Alex led the way down the stairs and did what he needed to get the job done. Focusing so he wouldn't trip, he counted carefully, "Hop, hop, hop!" with each step. He almost stole the show from the lovely bride, his new Aunt Suzanne. Almost. My nervous younger brother, the groom, said later that Alex saved him by clearing the tension and making him laugh.

Later during the reception, I gave my best-man speech and asked the guests to raise a glass to the new couple. As if on cue, Alex burst out, "Mommy, I've got to go wee-wee!" Forget the decorum and any seriousness that remained in the room. Alex was classic on that important day.

I recently came across those wedding photos, along with other pictures of family events. Putting this book together has driven me back down Memory Lane countless times. I should know that road perfectly by now, each mile marker as familiar as my sons' faces.

It isn't only photographs that remind me to look back. I hear the Dave Matthews Band on the radio and feel a bittersweet smile cross my face. It was one of Alex's favorites.

I watch *Gladiator* and know that Maximus's most searing pain came not from his loss of freedom nor the agonies of the Roman arena, but from his separation from his family, the horror of their deaths, and his inability to save them. I hear my favorite line and am reminded that I will meet Alex again, but "not yet. Not yet."

Then there's *Field of Dreams*, a father-son movie if ever there were one. I hear the line "Is there a heaven?" and the answer "Yes, it's where dreams come true," and I hope it is so.[2]

Just turning on the television can draw laughter because it reminds me of the time I caught a very young Alex watching something he might have been too young to see. It was suppertime one night, and Mindy already had the younger boys in their high chairs. When Alex didn't come when she called, I went in search of him. As I neared the den, I heard him say, "Ooh, baby!" He said it again, "Ooh, baby!" as I reached the room and saw women in scanty costumes dancing across the TV screen.

I hurried to turn it off before scooping him up and returning with him to the kitchen. I didn't stick around long enough to see what program it was. We didn't have any movie channels with little guys in the house, so it was likely some fairly innocent TCM musical with Bing Crosby, Frank Sinatra, or Tony Curtis. Still, I was no dummy and held off telling Mindy for fear of retribution (on me!). Eventually my big mouth got the better of me, and soon Alex became legendary for that story as well.

As a family, we shared countless touchstones that gave us a sense of togetherness, of having a place to roost. We mark our lives by these details, milestones in time that connect us. "Remember when . . ." becomes an anchor that assures us we're not alone, that we cherish others and are special to them too.

God, who is a community unto himself of Father, Son, and Holy Spirit, created us in his image to share life with one another.

We love; we argue; we celebrate. We become attached and grieve detachment. And all those events we mark by time, an elusive entity that drives us and holds us in bondage to some degree.

But we were not created to live within the limited realm of time. God made us for forever. Yet because we live on this bubble world of earth, it's easy to carry on as if life begins and ends here. Considering that most of us never experience anything beyond the few thousand feet of atmosphere that a commercial jet can reach, it isn't any wonder so many struggle to trust in the beyond.

When my father was diagnosed with leiomyosarcoma in January 1992, we knew it marked the beginning of the end of his time here with us, barring a miraculous cure. I fumed at the doctors who advised us to help him get his affairs in order in the next six weeks, telling them in no uncertain terms that they didn't know my dad. My boys were six, four, and three back then, and we all wanted them to grow up knowing him. He had so much to teach. Being raised within his influence was an immeasurable gift I wanted for them, and frankly I wasn't ready to let go of it myself.

He set a goal to see Alex graduate from high school, and he nearly made it. After battling the disease for twelve years, through numerous surgeries that kept him going but gradually reduced his lung capacity, his body finally had enough. He passed away in April 2004, weeks shy of Alex's graduation. The boys were eighteen, sixteen, and fifteen by then, and I'm so grateful they got to know their papa.

Life and death and the memories that happen in between: these boundaries characterize life here.

One Christmas break our family escaped the Illinois winter and traveled to Naples, Florida, with a couple of the kids' friends. My parents fell in love with the area long ago, my mother winters there each year, and we've been there yearly since the boys were tiny. With just a few steps we can take the boat out fishing from their dock or be on the short pathway to the beach.

We were always taking the boys' friends with us to Walker and Naples and felt fortunate to be able to hop on the Montgomery corporate jet and share those trips with other kids, some of whom had never been south or been fishing. My father especially enjoyed the activity of the young people as he fought his cancer battle.

During that particular Christmas visit, the kids wanted to parasail, so one afternoon we took turns flying above the waves. I watched as the boys went up in pairs, their toes pulled off the boat's deck to trail in the sky.

Anyone who has parasailed knows the silence of the ride. Except for the occasional shifting of metal and nylon equipment and the gentle tug of the wind, the air up there is still, unbroken. I witnessed my kids experience a kind of release from the antagonism of land. It's a different kind of freedom than can be found on the ground, unnerving in a way to feel abandoned by terra firma. But it does offer a thrill to be loosened from the earth's grip if even for a short while.

Yet as freeing as parasailing can be, the boys were still attached in some form to the here and now.

On a broader realm, for now we're limited by gravity, time, age, sin, choices of others, and history's effects. And even though we still have many questions about the here and now, it's familiar. We've never experienced anything else. We don't find comfort in what seems foreign or far away.

My experiences with Alex after his soul left him bridged

the gap between the present life and the one to come. I'd been taught to believe in a glorious next life; I'd even prayed for more faith. But my engineering mind had questions that had remained unanswered.

God familiarized me with his timeless world and brought me comfort through it. He showed me in the sixth message that he inhabits this world we're familiar with as well as the one to come that bewilders and sometimes frightens us. People can deny it, avoid thinking about it, attempt to run from it, or even curse it. But someday each of us will face it. Meanwhile, God employs unique methods to help us embrace it. And he longs for us to learn to be embraced *by* it. I felt embraced by it that day.

Without warning, I felt as if Alex and I were lifted above the scene of devastation. We hovered on a suspension bridge that spanned the distance from earth to heaven, much like a jungle rope bridge in movies.

I still held Alex, and we were looking down on our earthly bodies in his living room. As with the other messages, feelings of comfort and companionship flowed.

I felt as if we were surrounded by God and Jesus, and likely the Holy Spirit, who were helping me walk through this day. They offered their strength and, though not quite peace of mind, a sense of tranquility and calm.

The images flipped quickly, and the next moment I sensed Alex meeting his grandmother Barb, Mindy's mother, for the first time. Barb had died fourteen months before Alex was born, after waging a courageous five-year fight with cancer.

Cancer appeared to have won, but I knew from this vision that ultimately someone else won in her life. Feeling Alex connecting with this wonderful Carol Channing look-alike brought me as close to joy as I can describe for right then. The moment shone.

My dad and Mindy's father came next, followed by Alex's "jolly Uncle Josh," Mindy's brother who had died of type 2 diabetes two weeks after his thirtieth birthday, when Alex was three. Alex had always insisted he remembered Josh, but Mindy and I had had our doubts. Who's to say, though, all that God can plant in us as lifelong memories. He certainly was surpassing everything I'd assumed of him.

After that, I also sensed that Alex was greeting Mindy's and my grandparents and scores of people from history he'd studied in school.

Years of unanswered questions came together in those seconds. Although I didn't see Alex's meeting Barb, Josh, and the others in hi-def, I had the unmistakable understanding of it all on the bridge with Alex and the Godhead. It was enough to solidify my confidence that this meeting was taking place right then. I also knew that my boy was happy and free of pain, flashing his *Cool Hand Luke* grin.

To allow me to revisit other loved ones I missed was balm. God could have stopped the messages after only one or two or even five, but he kept them coming to include this one. He let me know that Alex was whole in the Lord's presence, and he was sharing eternity with others we had loved. I thought again what a good guy God is to bring the worlds together. He exchanged my understanding of a temporary, earthly life for a view of forever.

In him there is no such thing as good-bye. That's a promise I hold on to each minute. No good-byes in Jesus. Death does not have to be permanent. I will meet Alex and the others again, but "not yet. Not yet."

Who are we humans to assume that our limited experiences encapsulate everything that's real? Scientists, many of the most influential doubters of God, have claimed for years that we use only a fraction of our brains. Considering the mind-body-soul connection, there may be a case that Adam and Eve used a great deal more of what God built into them before sin maimed everything of earth. Who can say how closely their heavenly Father communicated with them before unholiness created the great divide? A divide that Jesus crossed by becoming the bridge that I stood on with my firstborn.

And consider the universe. Astronomers know that we've barely begun to explore its reaches. We can't see it all. But at the place of meeting God, we find asylum in the unknown.

I can't understand all God is or why he works as he does. I can't grasp an existence released from time, nor can I understand eternity previous to me and still to come. But I know he isn't bound by time or space. He manages the stretches I cannot.

While he isn't limited to time's restraints, neither is he unsympathetic to his creation that is. I believe he smiles over our joys just as he holds us during tearful times. He ministers to us when we're in limbo, waiting to reunite with our loved ones who've already gone ahead, yet still holding on to those we love here and the responsibilities he gives us until it's our own time to go.

I still have a stack of condolence cards that will age as years pass, though the kindness of their givers is timeless. I don't know the origin of the following poem, but it was written on one card:

The Little Ship

I stood watching as the little ship sailed out to sea. The setting sun tinted his white sails with a golden light. As he disappeared from sight a voice at my side whispered, "He is gone."

But the sea was a narrow one. On the farther shore a little band of friends had gathered to watch and wait in happy expectation. Suddenly they caught sight of the tiny sail and, at the very moment when my companion had whispered, "He is gone," a glad shout went up in joyous welcome, "Here he comes!"

Hanging on to Alex on the bridge, I didn't want to let go of time, but I also realized that I could live with his temporary absence because of eternity. I haven't really lost him at all, but I have to miss him awhile longer.

God is gracious to offer us salvation through his Son. But to favor us with hope and joy and a shared forever with those we've loved shows his enormous kindness. We don't have to say good-bye and grieve a final closure. We still grieve deeply, but the relief that it doesn't have to be final steadies us to live on the bridge.

When I focus on eternity with the Lord, my state of mind can be transformed. I am not the first to hear from him so clearly, but my story is sacred between God and me. This life that I live between two worlds is not easy. I still mark moments and milestones, and I smile over memories from when Alex was here with me.

And I thank the Ancient of Days and his Son for the bridge.

Chapter Eight

Reason to Hope

For this God is our God for ever and ever;
he will be our guide even to the end.

PSALM 48:14

$\mathcal{M}$emories can be a balm or betrayer. We love the good ones, but painful ones can cripple. Perhaps one reason the Lord met me in such life-affirming ways after Alex's death was so that when the questions refuse to relent and my peace feels scrambled yet again, I will remember how he whispered to my soul.

Remember, Al. Remember what I showed you.

The night before the six-month anniversary of Alex's death, I remembered. I dreamed that night, and although I'm not often able to recall details of my dreams, this one is still vivid years later.

I dreamed Alex and I were in a hotel room as guests of his best friend the night before his friend's wedding. Alex was to be his best man.

I remember being relieved that Alex was alive and with me, acting like his jovial self, but also recalling that something didn't seem quite right. My relief was gradually overtaken by worry, to the point that I insisted on sharing the double bed with Alex so as not to let him out of my sight.

He scolded, "Geez, Dad, I'm not five years old anymore. Just chill, okay, Al?" He flashed his trademark grin, as he always did when he called me by my first name.

My worry about his leaving, or not really being there, was assuaged momentarily by anticipation of the next day's events, being with our friends and family, a wonderful feeling that all was well again. For that moment I felt whole.

I got out of bed to get a drink of water from the bathroom and asked Alex if he wanted one.

"No, I'm fine, Dad. I'm going to sleep now. We've got a big day tomorrow." I watched him pull the covers over his shoulders, and then he turned on his side and looked very comfortable.

The cold water tasted great, and soon I turned off the bathroom light. I started back toward the bed but stopped quickly.

Alex was gone.

And then I woke up. Crestfallen, I felt as if my heart had been snatched from my chest. I was awake and back in reality.

My counselor tells me that we grieve in different ways, and I suppose this was one way my sorrow was showing itself. Perhaps the human need to keep hoping was shining through. The dream soothed me while my subconscious experienced my son alive, well, happy, and with me.

The dream took me back to the anchors God had given

me on the day of Alex's death and gave me similar comfort. Along with the previous six, I recalled this seventh message. It was probably the most soothing that October day because through it God reminded me that Alex was his.

Seeing Alex on the bridge between this life and the next, along with loved ones who welcomed him to the other side, provided some consolation, of course. But I'm grateful that God didn't stop there.

Each previous vision had been a building block, beginning with the image of Alex and Dad in the boat in Minnesota. With this new message he confirmed that Jesus had secured salvation for my boy when Alex had chosen him as a teenager.

This reminder is still key to knowing I wasn't concocting these messages on my own. A power far greater was nurturing these seeds of hope in the desert of grief. This one was the clincher that stopped the insanity so that God could give me real peace of mind.

Peace, real peace, came over me then. I remember saying to God, "Is that right?"

Yes, no doubt about it. Don't you remember?

During their teen years, my boys were involved in Young Life ministry, a parachurch organization that meets weekly under the direction of regional youth leaders. Teens from all over the area, from all sides of the tracks, can join together for Christian, faith-filled teaching and social time with peers. The leaders make it fun for them to learn about Jesus and what he means for them. Alex, Bryan, and Jimmy all took part in the Moline area YL group, led for more than forty years by my friends Jeff and Sue Tunberg.

Mindy and I were often a little worried about our first-born, not for anything he had done or would do, but because we were nervous, amateur parents giving it a go as best we knew how. Sure, we took all three boys to Sunday school and church consistently, but it was really through Young Life that Alex made his commitment to Christ. Alex's early foundation in church developed into his own faith during this season, and he made a decision to believe in Jesus as Savior one summer at a Young Life camp.

I saw his desire for a relationship with the Lord. His faith showed in his care for people and his goal to make the world a better place. Those attitudes weren't just born from being taught to serve. They came from a heart that had been touched by saving grace, a heart that had admitted its failings and need for redemption.

Jim and Jani Piercy sometimes took Alex and other students to church with them on Sundays during college, and then out for a nice dinner. Those four-hour returns to normalcy offered him some grounding while away from home during those years.

Alex's faith was reinforced by seeing it in action, by observing how the Piercys reached out to him and other college students by inviting them to church. Alex also saw that the Piercys were senior Bible Study Fellowship leaders in the community.

More than once as a young adult, Alex visited his Uncle

Chip and his family in their suburban Chicago home. Alex saw how Jim took his kids on mission trips and incorporated faith into everyday life. Jim's children are younger than mine, and as little ones, they absolutely adored my sons.

Jim chuckled as he recalled times when the situation was reversed and he had stayed with our family when Alex was two or three. Alex insisted that Uncle Chip sleep in the other twin bed in his room instead of in the guest room.

"Get in the alligator sheets," he'd prompt.

Still a couple of hours early for his own bedtime, Jim would play along and pretend to fall asleep—not easy with Alex giving him the eagle eye to make sure he didn't leave.

When Alex was thirteen or fourteen, Jim handed him the car keys one evening in Naples so they could go get ice cream.

"Huh?" Alex looked shocked.

"You drive."

"I have no idea how to drive, Uncle Chip!"

But he did fine and got a charge out of the adventure.

Another time when Alex was up in Walker with them, Jim sent him off to catch that night's supper. A little surprised initially, Alex worked hard all day and came back to the house feeling great about the stringer of fish he brought with him.

Jim looked forward to inviting Alex to be part of his men's Bible study group when Alex moved to the area after graduation, and Alex had shown interest in going with their family on future mission trips.

"He had so much going for him," Jim said. "He was a bright light. And he was funny, a prankster. But Illinois is a secular school, and like I had to, Alex had to work out his faith in that maze."

Like the rest of us, Alex didn't fit some human definition of a perfect Christian, as if there is such a thing. But his heart and soul belonged to Jesus. I wasn't around to monitor his every move, but I knew his character and his heart, and he was solid.

I like to think I showed him an example of grace that reflected God's own; I hope so, anyway. He was a great kid, and I didn't need to get on his case about much other than some smoking and underage drinking. The attitudes and actions that characterized him most were ones that mattered most—the ones that showed his heart of faith and care for others.

I hope I did enough right things as his father to give him a taste of the Lord's forgiving and accepting love. My own parents had given my sons and me that gift.

We took many trips with my folks to Florida, but another visit that stands out happened when the boys were about eight, six, and five. My dad wanted to take all three out fishing by himself, despite my warning. Papa thought it would be quality time with them. They loaded the gear into the boat and had backed away from the dock about thirty feet, when Alex ignored my father's instruction not to cast until he found a good spot. Alex let fly a cast and started reeling because he felt some tension and thought he'd hooked a big one. When Dad hollered in pain, Alex knew he had caught a 172-pounder.

Alex dropped the pole and saw the gash starting to bleed on the back of his grandfather's head. The two younger boys stood in shock, dutifully holding their poles steady.

Later, all three boys told me Dad didn't yell at all but calmly cut the line and told them to put away their poles at the back of the boat. Then he put the boat in reverse and went thirty feet back into the dock slip. Dad took the three bruisers back to the house and determined with Mom's help that he needed to go to the ER, even though a hospital was the last place he wanted to go right then. At that point he was well into his cancer fight but was on a break from chemo and radiation and was feeling pretty good.

Long story short, eight stitches later he returned. Alex had been crying, not because he had been scolded, but because he knew he had hurt his hero. As for me, I'll always be grateful to Dad for showing grace and not blowing up at my little guy. He modeled a quiet strength that looked like Jesus' character and drew others to him. He did add one more teachable moment a few days later, though, when he handed Alex the toenail scissors and tweezers to remove the stitches, illustrating that our actions create consequences. A loving grandfather showing the ramifications of a mistake.

I trust Alex's heart was blessed through other lessons of grace-filled faith that drew him to Jesus as he grew older.

That God reminded me of Alex's faith the day Alex died assured me of my son's welfare. Jesus' promise to forgive our sins when we trust him for salvation strengthened me because I knew Alex had done that. Without prodding from us, he had chosen to believe in Christ as a young teen.

After Alex died, Sue Tunberg found a response card that he had filled out at the end of a Young Life camp week. The cards helped staff gain insight into where kids were spiritually and how they could pray for the teens. The students could choose from a number of boxes to check depending on their interest or disinterest in learning more about Christ, their choice to accept him as Savior, or their prayer requests. Sue confirmed that Alex had checked the box acknowledging he had already made a commitment to Jesus.

God promises to fulfill our needs (Phil. 4:19). He proved that to me. I didn't have a lot of anger or rancor toward the Lord in those first moments—maybe those stages of grief just hadn't hit me. Whatever the case, I believe he covered me with his peace, love, and strength, much as he welcomed Alex into his rest.

The reason Alex is reunited with other loved ones is because of Jesus. It was as though God was following up the vision of Alex on the bridge with this proof, as if he was assuring me, *See, Al, this is why he's here with me now.* And in reassuring me regarding my son's faith, the Savior bolstered mine.

I felt the pieces come together. Alex and Dad in the boat, then the understanding that God held the last day of Alex's life as he had held all the others. Next, gratitude to have parented Alex for his lifetime, the importance of caring for people, God's heart as a Father, and crossing the bridge to the other side. These messages all led up to the confirmation that Alex is on the other side because of Jesus, the Bridge. It's possible I wouldn't have been so convinced of any of it without the logical flow of one assurance to the next. Putting them together, God expanded my previous scope of faith. The enemy may have won a battle in Alex's life in October 2008, but the war had already been won; Alex was God's forever.

I am apart from Alex for now, but he is all right. God knew he would take his life, and the Father's heart hurt for his pain as it does for mine. But he is still Lord of eternity and of my time-bound life on earth. He numbers my days and holds me through each moment. I remember the gift of fathering Alex and of God's promise of forever together for all who call him Savior. I can remember the Lord's care for people and do likewise. I can remember him beyond my questions. This is God's hope of heaven for me.

God's hope of heaven. On the worst day of my life, he defined it for me and dove into the depths of my terror to bring me back to a place where I could breathe. Working alongside the gift of memory, he sustains me with this hope. These messages are my reasons for continuing and even thriving. My hope is in heaven, and I know that that hope will not disappoint.

Chapter Nine

Giving Alex Back

[GOD] guards you when you leave
and when you return,
he guards you now, he guards you always.

PSALM 121:8 (MSG)

*A*fter comforting me with seven messages of hope,
the Lord gently spoke an eighth one. This one I
didn't like at all because it was the only one I'd known was
coming, and I dreaded it.

Alex still lay cradled in my lap as the messages morphed
together: me on the bridge with him, the joy of reuniting
with loved ones, the sureness of his salvation and eternal
life, my father and son pushing away from the dock as they
laughed without a care, memories of Alex's childhood, and
the promise that he was happy and healthy right then.

Jim Piercy and the authorities would be there soon.
These moments would be over forever. I was still in this
world trapped by time, and the minutes kept ticking against
my will. And then the eighth and final message that day:

Al, you have to give him back to me. It's time for me to take
him back.

How many ways are there to say no? If I refused enough times, might God acquiesce?

I felt my arms being loosened, and I could no longer hold Alex. Maybe I was tired and my muscles were cramping. Regardless, I believe God was releasing my grip, the only way I would have let go.

I dreaded making the calls I knew were necessary. I dreaded talking with the police and watching them turn this sacred cocoon into a cold and technical forensic investigation. They wouldn't understand, not enough anyway, that he was my *son*. This was not run-of-the-mill for me, as it may have been for them.

And then another scripture rang above my thoughts: "I go and prepare a place for you" (John 14:3). It had always been a favorite, but I fought it just then. Sometimes the Lord speaks difficult truth, and sometimes he speaks welcome truth at difficult times.

I looked at Alex's closed eyelids and committed to memory each detail of his face that I knew so well. Alex, Jesus, and I were back on the suspended bridge. The surreal atmosphere hovered as we stood between that moment and forever.

Alex and his Savior. The moment of meeting Immanuel, God with us, was at hand for my boy. It was time for them to go. Jesus led Alex, his arm draped over Alex's shoulder, and together they began their journey across the expanse. With each step they appeared smaller to me, but I understood they were closer than ever to each other. I couldn't hear if they were talking, couldn't see their faces, but I can imagine

Jesus' fulfilled promises lighting their countenances and their way. I watched them disappear from sight.

The doorbell rang.

I was back in the condo in central Illinois, and the authorities had arrived, along with Jim and his wife, Jani, and their pastor. The police did their thing and asked me the expected questions. I remember lashing back with words when one of them asked why I had taken down Alex's body. He was young. Maybe one day he will have a child and understand the offense of that remark.

They looked over Alex's body and throughout the unit. They checked his Blazer parked in front but didn't find any clues that led to a different conclusion than the obvious cause of death. No drugs or alcohol were found in him, and it was ultimately ruled a suicide.

Despite the one offensive question, the authorities were respectful and handled the situation well. After a while Jim and Jani drove me back to their home so the police and I could talk more comfortably. Just as I didn't remember running the length of the complex to the rear window where I first saw Alex, I didn't remember going to Jim and Jani's until several years later when they reminded me.

After the police and I were finally finished, I called Mindy's and my friends, Dwight and Donna Sivertsen, who agreed to drive to Mindy's work to be with her when I phoned with the news. They also drove with her to Augustana to offer support when she told Bryan and Jimmy.

I'm certain many other details of the day failed to stick

with me. When it was finally time to head home, Jim and Jani stepped in once more and would not allow me to make the drive myself. Spent, I laid down and slept some in the back of Jim's car while Jani followed in mine.

When we arrived in Moline, family and close friends were gathered at my mother's house and stayed late to grieve together and offer support. Several of those friends were parents from a playgroup Mindy and the boys had been in when the kids were very small. The shock shook us all as parents who'd grown together as our children had grown up.

Our immediate family spent the night, and after they went to bed around midnight I had some free moments to search the Psalms until I found verse 16 of chapter 139 about God's numbering our days before birth. He'd been faithful to raise the sun over each one of Alex's 8,345 days, and he'd seen Alex's eyes close in sleep as many times. He'd known the thoughts that thrilled him and the ones that brought him to his knees. As much as I still don't understand, I do know that God was faithful to my son, and I am learning to live forward, leaning into his faithfulness.

In the days following, I went to the coroner to pick up Alex's last effects, which were in a paper grocery sack stapled closed. I didn't open it. We planned the visitation and funeral. Mindy once commented about how much Alex loved our church that he and his brothers grew up in, just as I had grown up there many years before. First Congregational of Moline, Illinois, is a special place for us, so it was fitting that we held his memorial service there.

The visitation was packed. Every one of Alex's Logan Elementary School teachers from kindergarten through sixth grade came to say good-bye. It had been years since they'd been part of his life, but every one of them made the effort to be there. His fifth-grade teacher, Mr. Fitzpatrick—Mr. F— had been a favorite of Alex's, and I'll never forget him telling me, "I feel as if I've lost my future president." The eighty players on Jimmy's Augustana football team also came. They lined up in order of number, dressed to the nines, hair slicked back, handsome, courteous, wonderful support for Jimmy and for us.

The line at the funeral home sprawled some three to four blocks, many people waiting more than four hours to set foot in the building. My own cousin who was fighting bone cancer stood in line for two hours. Each face I saw that Sunday afternoon and evening will be framed in my mind for the rest of my life, and their collective kindness will carry me all my days. We were blessed by each one and the many stories of how Alex had touched a life or encouraged someone. If at my funeral I have even one-fifth of the crowd that honored Alex, I will feel I lived a meaningful life.

At the funeral service, Bryan and Jimmy spoke of their older brother with courage and love. Their cousin Ashley and Alex's friend Lars spoke as well, and I still don't know how all four made it through those eulogies.

All sixteen hundred people who attended heard comforting words from our longtime pastor. He spoke of the reality of brokenness and the fact that we don't understand ourselves sometimes. Yet we share our lifetimes with one another, and our precious memories can never be taken away. We can hold on to the promise that we're never alone, and we can live embraced by our faith.

Alex's body rests in a cemetery adjoining the park where all our boys swam and played many seasons of baseball. His grave is next to my father's folks' and twenty-five feet away from Mindy's grandparents'. The two sets of couples had been wonderful friends in the 1940s.

At the gravesite committal service, my minister, Rev. Dr. Mark Gehrke, provided a unique vision of hope. Mark has trained doves, and he released several at the gravesite. A lone one flew up to join two or three others high above us. Instead of focusing our gaze downward at the coffin going into the ground, he showed the hope of looking heavenward as we all witnessed the birds reunite in the big, beautiful sky.

At our reception at Mindy's house after the funeral, a young woman I remember as Katie from Kankakee approached me after everyone else had left. Quietly and sweetly she told me how Alex had reached out to her at Moline High. At the time, she was new at the school and likely looked somewhat lost when Alex picked her out of the packed hall. She had already spotted him by his laugh and the crowd around him.

She told me how honored she was to have him approach her, she thought initially, to ask her out. I recall she was blond, petite, and beautiful. But as I listened to her, I saw something more on the inside, something I suspect Alex sensed as well with his great people skills.

Alex simply asked where she was from and why she had recently shown up at the school. She told him sadly of her dad's job transfer. "He asked me what activities I had been involved in at Kankakee. I mentioned a few things, including the girls' tennis team.

"'Stop. Come with me,' he told me. Then he led me to a room where some MHS girls' tennis players were sitting prior to their next class."

Alex introduced her, and Katie explained that he magnified her résumé to the girls.

"Within a week he made me feel like I grew up there."

Her words didn't surprise me. In fact, they affirmed what I'd always observed about him. Alex in motion, making a difference.

Katie told me she not only went on to have a great tennis experience at Moline but she also enjoyed many fun student activities, including Young Life. She was so glad her dad and family were transferred there.

Gently but resolutely she concluded, "All my happiness at Moline High was because of Alex. I wanted you to know that, Mr. Hallene. I'm sorry for your loss. God bless you."

That conversation brings tears today. I don't recall Katie's last name, but her affirmation of Alex ranks near the top of my memories of those days.

My friend and former neighbor, Mary, is the mother of Alex's friend Alex Gloeckner, who went with us to Walker on that final visit in summer 2008. Her Alex was diagnosed with epilepsy when he was fourteen and was unable to drive as a result. She remembers how often my Alex called to offer her son rides to places, saving him the embarrassment of having to be driven everywhere by Mom. She confirmed what so many of us knew: "He was the nicest kid. I remember thinking that he gets it."

She also remembered whenever he'd come over to her house, he'd give her a big hug and call her Mama Glock. "He always made me feel good. In the days when my own kids were acting like wiry teens, it felt good to have a neighbor kid come over and give me a hug."

I'm sure not one person at his funeral could have predicted how Alex's earthly life would end. It didn't fit his personality or the way he lived. It was obvious that each of us knew we'd been separated from someone rare and special. I trust God continues to minister to each person who still mourns this life without Alex.

As hard as it was to live through, and still is, I think Alex's passing has been slightly easier on me than it has been on the rest of my family because of the time I had alone with him at the end. I wouldn't have wanted anyone else to find him.

I know Alex would want to encourage others, for he was a truly compassionate person, the go-to guy friends would often seek for counsel and comfort. I feel strengthened every day by this faith and thankful to have been the father to such a loving and sensitive young man.

One of Alex's favorite sayings was "It's go time or no time," and one day I will go and be with Alex and Jesus and never be separated again.

And so I gave him back to his eternal Father and his Savior, understanding that I can never actually lose him. This separation is temporary. I will always feel honored to have been Alex's earthly father, and I look forward to that day when I will be reunited with my little boy again. But not yet.

Until then, I ask the Lord to pass along my message to my firstborn: "Thank you, sweet prince, for being my great son. I adore you even more today than on the day you were born."

Chapter Ten

Hope Beyond Depression

He reached down from on high and took hold
of me; he drew me out of deep waters.
He rescued me from my powerful enemy,
from my foes, who were too strong for me.
PSALM 18:16–17

There's a scene in the 1990 film *Awakenings* when Robert De Niro's character, Leonard, urges Robin Williams's character to tell people about life. Second only to *Gladiator*, it's the movie that speaks most clearly to my hope of heaven.

"We've got to tell everybody. We've got to remind them how good it is."

"How good what is, Leonard?"

"Read the newspaper. What does it say? All bad. It's all bad. People have forgotten what life is all about. They've forgotten what it is to be alive. They need to be reminded. They need to be reminded of what they have and what they can lose . . . what I feel is the joy of life, the gift of life, the freedom of life, the wonderment of life."[3]

The movie is based on a true story of catatonic patients

who were temporarily pulled out of their isolation to enjoy life as they never had before. It shows not only the liberation of waking up to a new realm of wholeness but also how their awakenings changed the people around them for the good.

I want the good guy to win. I want to connect with others who yearn to be freed from mortality's trappings. Maybe that's why certain movies and songs stay with me, especially when their messages resonate with my story. The final scene of *Field of Dreams* gets me when the father and son reunite to play ball together. Others such as *Ghost*, *Shadowlands*, *Ordinary People*, and *Meet Joe Black* let me know I am not alone in my longing for an afterlife that sets right our broken places.

On a larger, theological scale, God has changed me. More than five years since the day I witnessed God's eight messages, I continue to be awakened to his movements. With that awakening, the memories continue to come, a mixed bag of bittersweet. There's enough to process for eternity, and the more I process, the more I want to spend this passing time telling others about the future God has planned.

During the writing of this book, I visited Alex's grave on the fifth anniversary of his death. Autumn had arrived in Illinois. In Riverside Cemetery, procrastinating leaves clung to branches overhead. Others rested on gravestones or lay trampled underfoot along pathways that wove through rolling acres.

I never stay long. I simply put three yellow roses of Texas

on his grave and say the Lord's Prayer. Yellow roses have become symbolic for me, as Alex and Bryan were born in Texas, and we knew Jimmy was on the way before we moved from there back to Moline years ago. Placing those roses on Alex's grave has become a tradition several times a year: on his birthday and death day, Mother's Day, his mother's birthday, and Father's Day.

Several weeks later we honored his twenty-eighth birthday on Thanksgiving, just as we did on the day of his birth in 1985. I figured on the calendar that it was the fifth time his birthday fell on that holiday, the first since his death. Jimmy's birthday was the following day, but that year we celebrated his on Thanksgiving. I'm not sure we'll do that frequently, because Jimmy deserves an unencumbered birthday, but it was a super day, and we were able to acknowledge Alex without dwelling on his absence. We watched Bryan's Dallas Cowboys and ate cake, and the three of us went to the cemetery together, said the Lord's Prayer, and placed another trio of roses.

Before long, Christmas came, then another new year. Time continues to roll while I continue to process.

I have several of Alex's birthday celebrations on DVD, my homegrown movies. Seeing him in motion and hearing his voice keeps the memories ever-present. Even though the years I was given to raise him were not enough, they provided a continual stream of remembrance.

I can put in a DVD and see him turn one and then three years old all over again, my little boy quickly growing into my young man. He was one cute kid, especially when stuffing his cheeks with cake, oblivious that he was the center of attention. Mindy was approached more than once in the grocery store by people telling her he could have been a baby model.

I can revisit Alex at eight years old, with friends at his gymnastics birthday party, thanking each giver as he opened presents. Life pulsed through him as he ran and jumped and joked and did all the things boys do. The memories are real enough that I can almost feel the crispness of the air that day. It was sweatshirt weather, and he wore a navy one. I wonder how many team sweatshirts he wore from the time he was six months old: Moline, Walker, University of Illinois, take your pick of Chicago's pro teams.

The years zoomed by and then came his seventeenth birthday. The breeze off the Gulf in Naples rustled the palm leaves. I recall the air was warm, as was the sight of my sons and relatives gathered poolside for cake and gifts. Again I hear Alex's voice and the sounds of easy conversation and family life.

I kept a recording of his voicemail greeting so I could hear the carefree sound of him. With a couple clicks of technology, I can relive the days when Alex was happy and healthy and celebrating growth.

It is a mystery to me when the seeds of depression first planted themselves in him. Science tells us some people are more prone to chemical imbalances than others. Heredity can play into it, and it may have done so in Alex's case.

Stress, distress, grief, or any number of triggers can tip the scales of our brain chemistry.

Sometimes depression comes on like a slow drain, difficult to discern that it's happening. We adjust to a new normal that feels a little lower than it used to, and we vaguely remember being a more upbeat person. Days lag, energy lags, smiles become forced, until one day someone close to us suggests we get help. They see we are trapped. That is, if the signs are visible. Other people wear the mask, as my doctor calls it, like an expert, as Alex did.

I don't know how Alex's depression came on, gradually or with force. I don't know what instigated it or how long he really struggled.

In my case, nearly three years after Alex passed away, the illness hit like a Mack truck and took me down hard and without warning. I thought I'd been grieving, but this was an entirely new phase.

Prior to then, in the immediate days after Alex passed away, I had gone into protector mode. I continued to feel my own sorrow, but I poured my time and thoughts into seeing to the rest of my family. Everywhere I looked, I saw bruised hearts and vulnerable emotions, and as a dad, son, and friend, I felt drawn to help everyone else.

And then in the summer of 2011, Alex was named honorary late best man at the wedding of his lifelong best friend. The weekend was a wonderful time, and I was not sad. Films of the groom and Alex played tastefully throughout the rehearsal dinner and reception. Joyful memories. But my focus kept returning to the word *late* by his name on the program, and I was struck by Alex's obvious absence. It was an event he never would have missed, but he wasn't there, and something clicked: Alex was gone. He really was gone from the earth. I'd known it. I'd lived it. I'd survived it thus far. But reality hit deeper that evening.

My counselor says mine is a complicated grief. Having someone die of suicide in itself can bring forth complicated grief, but being witness to it creates a much more severe form of distress. And when it was someone so young, particularly my own child—whom I thought was doing fine and wasn't exhibiting any signs of depression—all those elements took me beyond grief to trauma. It finally hit me with all its post-traumatic power.

In her article "A New Normal: Ten Things I've Learned about Trauma," Catherine Woodiwiss stated that trauma permanently changes us, but that isn't a wholly negative thing. Suffering through trauma alone is unbearable. Healing is seasonal, not linear. Love shows up in unexpected ways. And we need to allow those suffering to tell their own stories, meaning each individual needs to discover hope in his or her personal situation. She also defined two groups of people who help us through trauma. She called them firefighters and builders. Firefighters arrive on the scene for immediate help and rescue, whereas builders are those who stay with us for the long haul and help us heal.[4]

When post-traumatic stress arrived on my doorstep, I needed to shut down for a while. I took a leave of absence from my teaching position and moved in temporarily with my mother, a "builder," and the person I needed most during those four months. I was in so much turmoil that I lay on her couch throughout the day, poring through the Psalms when I felt able. My mother is like gentle steel. She is a gem, and she and the Lord saw me through that time.

It took awhile for the doctors to get my medication regulated. I was on the wrong one initially, and I struggled with unusual side effects, such as palsy. My muscles would give out suddenly, and I'd collapse.

When I was convinced I couldn't get off the couch, Mom would ask if I'd seen my doctor and taken my medication. She pushed me to take walks around the neighborhood, somehow knowing the movement and fresh air would help keep me going. At first it was tough to make it down the block to the neighbors' house, but consistency built my endurance, and I'm up to five miles several times a week now.

A few friends also built into me, refusing to let me isolate too much. My friend Chris often called to say, "I'll pick you up at quarter to seven for Bible study." When I'd reply no, he'd answer, "Okay, ten to seven."

The Sivertsens, who had been a support to Mindy and me by going to her office the day of Alex's death, called weekly. "We'll pick you up at 6:15 to go to Ming Wah's for supper. . . . No? Okay, we'll see you at 6:20."

Somehow I knew all along that I would be okay, and I never felt the desperation of suicidal feelings, but I did not feel good and knew it would be a long haul to recovery. I knew I was still sick when I really worried because my mom went away for a few days.

I did travel on my own to Naples for three weeks and immediately felt somewhat better, going from the dark, cold northern weather to the warmth of the sun and invigorating swims. In the last months of his life, Alex had taken up swimming as well, and I've wondered if he was using the exercise to get his endorphins flowing.

In time, my doctor and my counselor deduced some reasons for my post-traumatic stress, guilt being a primary one. Having dealt with bouts of depression personally several times, I couldn't get over the fact that I hadn't seen the signs in my child. I had become so familiar with them in myself and in others, but his mask was so effective that no signs were visible to me, or to anyone else as far as I know.

The full force of the trauma I'd experienced upon discovering his body lay dormant for three years, but my ongoing grief did show in my inability to rest regarding the safety of my other loved ones. For two years I'd call Bryan and Jimmy at Augustana at ten o'clock each night to make sure they were okay. I regret doing that, but again, my subconscious was in a level of turmoil I didn't know about yet. I also slept with my cell phone mere inches from my head to ensure I wouldn't miss another late-night call.

At first I hid the true method of Alex's suicide from Mindy, my sons, and my mom to protect their feelings. I told them he had overdosed on generic aspirin, which seemed gentler than the rope.

I even created a new death certificate when Mindy asked to see it at the end of that year. I whited out parts of the original and copied it, and then I found the matching font and typed in my made-up cause of death by aspirin overdose.

I felt great compassion for her because she had carried Alex inside of her. As his mother, she had cradled his heart as no one else had, and I worried the reality would be too hard on her. She figured it out, however, and eventually pulled the truth from me, acknowledging that it was a kind gesture on my part. I've realized since then that I suffered uniquely as well, having been the only one to witness the harshness of his death.

Then years later, on the night of his friend's wedding when I saw the word *late* in reference to Alex, my subconscious finally realized he had died. My counselor said my mind had buried the reality all that time. While I was working so hard to protect others, I unwittingly had been protecting myself too.

We've surmised that my attempts to cover up the way Alex died might have even anchored and prolonged the denial stage of grief in my subconscious, deeply enough that I might have denied his death.

I'd had three previous situational episodes of depression, fortunately not a life plagued by them. Knowing him as I did, I believe Alex's life was not characterized by repeated bouts either. I didn't struggle with it early in life, when I was so active as a competitive swimmer and a jogger for more than forty years. But after sports-related injuries and several surgeries forced me to reduce my physical activity, my brain struggled to keep those vital chemicals flowing as I needed.

The first time I dealt with depression, job pressures brought it on after our move to Texas. I had walked into a tumultuous situation at work, into circumstances that set me up to fail. The previous person in my new role had been fired, and I, the boss's son, seemed like an outsider. I didn't have the help necessary to turn things around, we lacked staff, and the stress was intense. I'm talking stress along the lines of having thirty or forty elevators behind four to six months, with the governor arriving the next day. I'd had some pretty tough jobs previously, but this pressure exceeded them all.

I couldn't sleep, a problem I had never experienced, and I began to have anxiety attacks. Unaccustomed to it all, I felt incredible fear of the unknown and fear that I couldn't cut it. I was only thirty-two, but I felt the weight of the world like a much older man.

The emotions took me back to college when I wondered if I could cut it at Illinois. I remembered that my roommate and I each had a copy of the same chemistry book, but he would tear out sections of his after reading it, because he had mastered the information and he wanted to make the book lighter to carry. I, on the other hand, didn't have such an easy time.

Add to that, I was giving Mindy shots to help us get pregnant, and her mother had died, so both of us were grieving.

After four months or so, it all got to me. I felt embarrassed going to a psychiatrist and taking medication for anxiety and depression. However, those supports helped me recover. Eventually the difficult transition improved, we raised productivity 200 percent at work, and the experience became a highlight of my career. And Mindy and I got pregnant.

From that time, I learned two things: to hang on and believe that things can improve, and to detect the signs of depression and anxiety, certainly in myself but in others too.

Then in 1999 I struggled with the divorce and spent time at Mayo Clinic, which helped me to identify a solution to get back up and running. Then for several months from late 2006 to early 2007, I went through a delayed reaction to my father's death in April 2004. The distress of those months rolled into great concern for Alex after his cry for help in the summer of 2007, following the incident with his grandmother's car in Florida. And then, of course, my worst battle with depression came in 2011, prompted by October 2, 2008.

I've learned a great deal about how we process grief and other emotions and how those can play into depression. From my physician and my counselor, I've learned that the brain's cortex, necessary for mature, adult-like reasoning, isn't fully developed until the late twenties. Considering that children are magical thinkers, we naturally come to adulthood with some false beliefs and inadequate processing of life. We bring two decades of mixed messages from others, plus the enemy's lies, into our grown years.

In Alex's case, his depression may have been influenced in part by his age. The twenties can be a vulnerable decade because the brain isn't cognitively complete. Add those physical complexities to the pressures of measuring up, the desire to prove oneself and to matter in the world, along with the critical decisions about relationships and career and finances and independence, and it's a big load to haul. No wonder life can feel overwhelming.

If depression does result, irrational beliefs from childhood can be refocused, as can beliefs about ourselves and how to process our place in life. Cognitive therapy can help retrain habitual processing habits that steer us wrong. Other times medication is helpful. Awareness of the potential for depression and its warning signs, along with keeping tabs on our kids' stress levels, is a maintenance role for parents.

As a Native American saying goes, "It isn't the pain that is the problem; it is our resistance to the pain that causes suffering." We must deal with the issues and not shy away because of old-school stigmas about depression or misguided ideas that more faith ought to be enough to suck it up and keep going.

Absolutely, faith in the Lord provides an advantage. We need it like air and water, our lifeline. He carried me from one breath to the next during my toughest times. But when someone suffers from clinical depression, denying the need for medical help is similar to refusing medical treatment for cancer because enough trust in God ought to heal it. Clinical depression is a medical illness, not a shortage of faith.

According to my counselor, depression symptoms are often more visible in women than in men. Younger men in particular don't always exhibit the typical signs. And we all respond differently to circumstances; stress for one person may show up physically, while in others it may reveal itself as depression.

As a society, we need to grow our understanding of how widespread depression is. The increase in suicide rates is attention-grabbing.

In its November 25, 2013, issue, *Time* magazine published an article on the people who answer calls through the National Suicide Prevention Lifeline network. It stated that suicide rates have been increasing since 2005. The most recent year of available statistics was 2010, when 38,364 Americans killed themselves, according to the Centers for Disease Control and Prevention. And that number includes only the ones that were recorded. Here are a few other statistics given:

- The National Suicide Prevention Lifeline expected 1.2 million calls in 2013.
- The number of calls has been increasing 15 percent every year.[5]
- Approximately one hundred million Americans (about one in three) are afflicted with depression.

Those are alarming facts. If accurate, then one out of every three people we see today is struggling with this potentially deadly invader. Even slight depression can decrease quality of life.

But God's message is one of hope. It's a hope of complete recovery, with proper medical care and the other components of good health, such as diet, exercise, sleep, and faith in a Father who claims the role of our healer (Ps. 103:1–3).

As I discovered, the study of the revelations in the book of Psalms pulled me out of despair, as they did for the people who wrote them long ago. While I was recovering, I found more than one hundred sets of verses in the one hundred fifty chapters of Psalms that deal with depression, distress, despair, and anger. These were written thousands of years before modern medicine and psychiatry, and they helped me realize for the first time that God knows me, he really loves me, he will stay with me, he will not let me perish, and he will restore me.

King David and the other psalmists had no trouble asking God why or admitting to weakness and doubt. Maybe the key to their questioning is that in their doubts and negative emotions they leaned in to the Lord for power.

I trust that God is okay with our questions, even our doubts and anger, when we take them to him. King David filled his psalms with every emotion he felt, and God called him a man after his own heart. The Lord understands more than we do how much we need him, and he's okay with that. He's even good with it. We need to get good with it, too, if we're to experience his hope that carries us.

David may not have felt like the embodiment of trust as he poured out his grievances to the Lord. But then again, maybe he understood that questions don't mean a lack of belief when we look to God with them; maybe they help grow honest, tenacious trust.

My counselor described grief like ocean waves. When a big wave looms, the worst thing we can do is tighten and resist. If we go with it, we'll end up less harmed. Grief can involve many waves, and as we go with them, as we embrace the pain, we find healing in the process. We're wired for survival to avoid pain, but God tends to work best in us through our suffering.

Our heavenly Father sees our faith as it's buffeted by waves of grief, and weathered faith is a thing of beauty. Rare.

At the bottom of some lakes not unlike our Lake May, petrified tree stumps still stand, though covered by waves. Pretty much nothing is going to take down those fossils. They've become unbreakable through the weathering. They show signs of wear and tear, but they are more solid than rock. Faith is like that.

God wants us to expect that he'll minister to us. He showed me that hope beyond depression is possible. I experienced it, and my son is with its Source today. Jesus, that Source, walks with us here, meets us on the bridge, and sees us home.

Chapter Eleven

Until We Meet Again

I cry to you, LORD; I say, "You are my refuge,
my portion in the land of the living."
PSALM 142:5

Recounting October 2, 2008, has brought great heart-ache, but my son brought so much joy. I smile to remember him, and I can't end on anything but talking about him on a positive note. I'm going to tell how God has continued to remind me of his eight messages, but first I want to tell about one of Alex's roommates.

During a visit to Alex his sophomore or junior year at Illinois, I was introduced to a duck he'd brought home to live with him. He and his human roommates had noticed the baby bird wandering around the condominium complex, lost from its mother or booted from the nest. Being late fall, it was getting cold, so the guys brought the animal inside. They "found" (I didn't ask specifics) the oval top of a birdbath and filled it with water. They placed it on a blanket on which they wrote *Donnie Duck*, added chicken wire to create a pen, and nursed the duckling back to health.

When I asked how they'd known what to feed it, Alex

said they did some research and tried to emulate what the duck should have been eating in the wild. Then he added with a mischievous smile that Donnie also liked their table scraps, hamburgers, Doritos, and even a little beer once in a while.

I asked about the noise that could annoy neighbors or, heaven forbid, attract the attention of the condominium manager. Apparently Donnie was a quiet enough resident that he didn't disturb the peace.

The guys even had a leash and small dog collar so they could walk him outside for exercise.

"The girls love it, Dad," Alex said with a grin.

By then I was laughing, so any explanation would have sounded reasonable. That was my Alex: funny, goofy, yet honestly caring. Later when the duck was stronger and the weather warmed, they released Donnie by a lake outside town.

I love that he cared for something small and weak. He made time when many people wouldn't have bothered offering more than a "that's too bad" expression.

Recently, my Sunday school class looked at the derivations and meanings of some famous names from the Old Testament. Out of curiosity, I googled *Alexander* and found that it's originally from Latin and then Greek, and it means "defender, protector of man." This applies to my Alexander—at least as the protector of younger brothers and cousins, and even young ducks. Incidentally, *Alan*, a derivative of Alexander, seems appropriate for me, as I am the defender and protector of Alexander Montgomery Hallene and all he stood for and would have stood for.

As only someone who has been touched closely by suicide can understand, it breaks me wide open to hear suggestions that the Alex I knew *gave up* or *chose* to end his life. There are no words to speak strongly enough against this misconception. My Alex never gave up. He was a warrior who was brought down temporarily by the enemy of his soul and a physical illness. The enemy loves to use depression to sideline anyone he can reach.

In Alex's own strong mind that I knew for twenty-three years, he never would have chosen to take his life. He lived with passion and kindness and energy. He loved life and never would have grieved his family by leaving as he did. He was a protector, a caretaker, a watchtower for others.

But he suffered an illness that so many suffer from each day, people who need understanding and help as much as he did. That was my Alex, and I believe my purpose from here on is to fight for his memory and for the benefit of others who battle depression.

As for me, in the aftermath of Alex's death I felt God's protection in some very personal ways. I look back and see how he has been preparing me for a fresh vision. I can sense him guiding me daily with a special purpose that he's growing from my heartache.

During the first weeks after the funeral, I avoided people. While grateful for their expressions of care, I was overwhelmed. I had been uplifted by the outpouring of love and affection at Alex's visitation and funeral, but afterward I struggled being seen and consoled as a victim.

I couldn't read the dozens of grief books people had given as gifts. I couldn't go to church for several weeks out of fear of being approached and comforted. Many people were ready to help, but I needed aloneness. I craved anonymity in a town where so many knew and cared for us. Their faces reflected their grief, whose source was the same as mine, but I didn't think it could match the depth of mine. I didn't know how to comfort them as they sought to comfort me, and it was heartbreaking to see Alex's young friends together, because he was no longer with them.

But in those early days, I started to hear soothing church music the moment I woke up, then throughout the long days, and finally as I laid my head down to sleep.

I have always loved the old hymns from my childhood at First Congregational. A few days after the memorial service, I started to hear regularly the tune of a hymn that brought peace, but I wasn't familiar with it. I must have heard it before, but I couldn't place the name or remember the words.

I didn't think much about it except that God must have been sending his love and peace to me again. A month rolled by, and I finally went back to church on November 5, All Saints Day, when churches around the country honor the members who have passed away during the past year. As the service concluded, the choir began the closing hymn. I recognized the song that had played in my mind all month.

For all the saints, who from their labors rest,
Who thee by faith before the world confessed.
Thy name, O Jesus, be forever blest.
Alleluia! Alleluia!
Thou wast their rock, their fortress, and their might;
Thou, Lord, their captain in the well-fought fight;
Thou, in the darkness drear, their one true light.
Alleluia! Alleluia![6]

Tears flowed through three more stanzas, and I had to leave the service. This song had been a companion that had nudged me awake, accompanied me through each day, and tenderly put me to bed each night.

Time continued, and Easter 2009 arrived, our first without Alex. For almost their entire lives, our boys had spent the Easter week of no school with Mindy and me along with my parents at their winter home in Naples, Florida. Despite our loss weighing heavily on us during this sacred season, we were able to enjoy the ocean, the golf course, and seafood dinners at our favorite restaurants.

I was doing okay at church on Easter Sunday, and then the choir and brass quartet played the final hymn, "Christ the Lord Is Risen Today." Again, tears flowed throughout the four-verse hymn. I didn't want my sons or Mindy or Mom to see me crying, so I turned toward the aisle to dry my eyes.

As I kept my eyes closed to minimize my tears, the choir and quartet went into the benedictory response of Handel's *Messiah*, and I saw him. Alex was singing joyfully in a white choir robe with a white shirt and tie. All white and surrounded by fellow heavenly choir members. It was a reminder that Alex worshiped Jesus in person on his first Resurrection Day in glory. I celebrated a lot of firsts with him, but that's got to top them all.

Again overcome, I had to wait for my family at the back of the church.

In the next three and a half years, four more hymns became meaningful to me at my home church, Moline Faith Lutheran. Each one overwhelmed me to the point that I had to leave the pew. Each reminds me that God was near in October 2008, and he remained by my side.

In 2009, the hymn was "Here I Am, Lord." Here are the final lines:

> *I will give My life to them.*
> *Whom shall I send?*[7]

Then in 2010, "Spirit of God, Descend Upon My Heart":

> *Spirit of God, descend upon my heart;*
> *Wean it from earth; through all its pulses move;*
> *Stoop to my weakness, mighty as thou art,*
> *And make me love thee as I ought to love.*[8]

Another year passed, and 2011 brought "Love Divine, All Loves Excelling":

Love divine, all loves excelling,
Joy of heaven, to earth come down,
Fix in us thy humble dwelling;
All thy faithful mercies crown!
Jesus, thou art all compassion,
Pure, unbounded love thou art;
Visit us with thy salvation;
Enter every trembling heart.[9]

And then 2012 arrived. As usual, one Sunday morning like so many others, I took my place in church. Midway through the service, the organ peals rang out the Communion hymn. I was familiar with this one; in fact, "Shall We Gather at the River?" is a personal favorite. I thought nothing of it and began to sing while I waited to go up and kneel at the altar to take Communion.

All of a sudden, I started to weep. Unable to stop, I wondered what was the deal.

Then I realized that my last favorite picture of Alex showed him with his hands raised, holding a bottle of wine, relaxed and comfortable outside in a deck chair. He smiled at the camera. That picture was taken weeks before he died, late in the summer of 2008. He was at his late grandpa Grafton's summer home in Muscoda, Wisconsin, mere feet from the Wisconsin River. Although I wasn't with him on that trip, as a family we had gathered at that river many times.

For the sixth time, I had to withdraw from the sanctuary to avoid concerned looks.

The most recent song came in March 2013. That spring day I spent several hours typing and editing a summary sheet for speaking engagements when I talk to groups about the Lord's messages to me. When I clicked Print at last, the old Roy Rogers song "Happy Trails to You, Until We Meet Again" began in my head.

> *Happy trails to you, until we meet again.*
> *Happy trails to you, keep smilin' until then . . .*[10]

The rest of the song faded into my tears. I hadn't heard it in probably fifty years, but it was no coincidence that it played just then. The tune has a soothing quality about it. Nothing complex, but there's a peace in its lyrics and tone. When Dale Evans Rogers wrote it back in 1950, the Lord saw the day it would remind me that I'd see my child again.

I have been protected through this journey in ways I haven't always welcomed but are evident nonetheless.

I will smile to remember Alex's life. I will smile at the grace shown to me upon his death. My glimpse into heaven prompts me to pray that others will experience God's gifts of grace as well, suited to their needs. His grace brings me back from despair and reminds me that I am still here for a reason. He has a special purpose for my life, through all its heartaches and joys.

Over my lifetime, both of my parents encouraged me

that I was special because I had been nearly dead at birth. I was more than a month premature, and my lungs weren't fully developed yet, a virtual death sentence back in those days. Both sets of my grandparents drove down to Oak Ridge, Tennessee, to be with my twenty-two-year-old parents while their baby—me—died. I spent twenty-eight days in an incubator, and my mom said she was the only mother in the hospital who wasn't allowed to hold her baby, much less take me home. My folks spoke from the heart when they reminded me that life is a gift. Ever since I was about five years old, I recall their telling me that I had been allowed to live for a unique purpose. I've been given more than sixty extra years so far.

I have always felt self-imposed pressure to make something of my parents' words, and I know Alex put that pressure on himself as well, as he had almost died at birth too.

Of course, no matter what circumstances greet a child entering the world, he or she is special simply as God's creation. Yet the import of my parents telling me they believed God had a role suited for me has stuck with me and driven me to pay it forward. I saw in Alex that same desire to make a difference.

So what's next? It's go time or no time, as Alex would have said. In *Gladiator*, Maximus sent his troops into battle with the charge that "what we do in life echoes in eternity."[11] It's now or never to press forward and help others.

Of course, my first priority is to be a father for my two sons. They have grieved deeply. They are two-thirds of my three bruisers; they knew Alex in ways I did not, as a brother. They share memories of him that are unknown to me, moments together as growing boys, adolescents, and young men. Yes, Mindy and I lost our son. Mom lost her grandson. But Bryan and Jimmy have more years ahead without Alex on earth, and they lost their leader, their compatriot, their colleague. I want to ensure their years are meaningful with joy and hope. They are keeping on with life, victoriously. Bryan works in accounting in Chicago and is studying for his CPA exams, and Jimmy is back in Moline working in sales. Their faith is strong, and I couldn't be prouder of them.

As a family, we've individually and collectively had to figure out how to move forward with all the things we do as a family—holidays, birthdays, traditions. The transition is a process as we discover and settle in to a new rhythm.

I continue to teach at St. Ambrose University in the College of Business. And in addition to being a support to others affected by Alex's death, I will continue with several other endeavors. Our family established a yearly scholarship to the University of Illinois available to a Moline High student. Alex had felt fortunate, yet guilty and discouraged for a friend from home who couldn't return to Illinois after his freshman year because his multiple scholastic scholarships covered only the first year. We have made sure that the scholarship in Alex's honor is good for four years, $2,500 a year, as long as the winner maintains at least a 3.0 average. In May 2014, we awarded the fifth annual Alexander Montgomery Hallene scholarship to a student in financial need. A plaque listing each year's winner and year is displayed outside the principal's office to inspire all twenty-four hundred Moline High students to pursue their dreams. The day after school lets out, each winner also receives a smaller plaque and a good deal of Illini memorabilia, including an orange hoodie of course, in a small, private ceremony with only our families present.

I am also creating the Yalex Foundation, which will serve several purposes that can expand with time:

1. To help people with depression
2. To offer recreational help for special-needs children and young people like my nephew Matt
3. To help feed hungry children
4. To help our veterans

The foundation and its website will help direct people to proper state and federal resources, such as the American Foundation for Suicide Prevention (AFSP). If the Yalex Foundation can help at least one person back off the ledge, or help one person from going out onto the ledge, or convince one person of God's love so he or she never goes out on the roof, then it will be worth the effort.

I also have ideas for developing an on-campus triage concept for university settings in Alex's honor. My thoughts are that these can be settings where students (or veterans) could enter without fear or embarrassment to receive academic or career counseling, as well as emotional counseling.

They could meet with doctors or counselors to gauge their needs and ascertain whether they are at risk for suicide. If necessary, an order would be sent to the dean that the patient is to be granted a leave of absence so he or she can avoid taking his or her life, and instead, take advantage of the time to recover and either resume his or her studies or pursue a different plan. If Alex had felt he had that option, who knows if he would be alive today.

I will continue to develop my speaking ministry to churches and other groups. The focus of my talk is to broadcast the hope and assurance of heaven, to help others see that God is too nice a guy not to have created a plan for us to reunite with those we've been temporarily separated from on earth. I pray this book will help many people, but it has been torture to write. I'm a people person; I love to communicate and connect in person. Speaking energizes me, and I feel it is my most effective way to reach out to others since it is comfortable and not invasive.

I will always be grateful to my mom, my sons, my counselor, the Sivertsens, and my friend Chris for encouraging me to get this book published. What began as a few thoughts that I scribbled out seven weeks after Alex passed away has become *The Hope of Heaven*.

When she encouraged me to pursue this, my counselor added that I needed to be honest about the way Alex had died. I struggled for two years with that advice, wondering whether I would be doing right by Alex's memory. I felt mad at God as I battled the understanding of what a gift these eight messages were, yet they seemed to come with a burden to share my son's personal story. I believe these truths are biblical and transferrable to others. Even now I pray it will be worth it, that the help I believe this story can be for others will far outweigh the pain, that my efforts to honor his legacy will ensure that he did not die prematurely in vain.

Ironically, the day I first put those eight messages on paper was November 22, 2008, the forty-fifth anniversary of the death of President John F. Kennedy, a longtime hero of mine. I was ten and in fifth grade when he saved, in my opinion, half of our country's lives through his cool and intelligent solving of the 1962 Cuban Missile Crisis. His words echo in my heart, and I pray they come through in this book:

> For, in the final analysis, our most basic common link is that we all inhabit this small planet. We all breathe the same air. We all cherish our children's future. And we are all mortal.[12]

And these as well:

> With a good conscience our only sure reward, with history the final judge of our deeds, let us go forth to lead the land we love, asking His blessings and His help, but knowing that here on earth, God's work is truly our own.[13]

However many days the Lord has counted out for me, I will share the promises he made to me—to us—thousands of years ago and each moment of our lives. He knows and loves each one of us, he will protect us, he will never forsake us, he will hear us when we call to him, he will strengthen us, and he will preserve us. He is our rock, our fortress, our deliverer, our shield, our stronghold, and our help. He is our light and salvation; he will restore us from our bed of illness; he will sustain us on our sickbed; he will uphold all those who fall and lift up all who are bowed down. He will be our guide even to the end. He is compassionate and gracious; he forgives our sins and heals our diseases; he heals the broken-hearted and binds up our wounds. And finally, he will keep us from all harm and watch over our lives, no matter what circumstances look like right now.

God has shown me through several events and people that he often works most powerfully in ways the visible world thinks of as backward. Maybe that's part of what makes the duck story so sweet. Alex took time to build up a small, overlooked, insignificant bird. In doing so, he added to the healing side on the scale of life.

What begins as small or weak God wants to grow into something mighty for his purposes. He saved two small Hallene babies, but never did I think that he could work through my son's death to birth a more alive faith in me. But our God loves to work that way. To show his control over death, maybe; to share his surpassing love, definitely.

As I grieved my late son, God spoke life to my heart and reminded me that he had been there for me since birth, just as he is for my children.

As Isaiah said, "For as the heavens are higher than the earth, so are My ways higher than your ways and My thoughts than your thoughts" (55:9 NASB). His thoughts are not limited as ours are. His methods are beyond ours for creating "beauty instead of ashes" (61:3). For his recreating power we can be so grateful, and we can choose to pass along his hope as we hold fast to him.

But he also understands that sometimes we don't have the strength to hold fast with faith. When pain rips to the point that we can't cling anymore, that's when he can reveal that *he* holds *us*, that his power and hope pull us through. He reaches to the bottom for us because he knows we cannot always reach any higher on our own. He is holding us even when we can't see him. Throughout Alex's life the Lord held him, even when I couldn't. And when Alex died, the Lord gave me a vision of his grace that sustained me as I struggled to keep hold of the boy I felt I had lost.

Hope in despair, beauty from ashes, working through the weak, methods that seem backward—all are signs of God's personal presence in each of our lives.

I've been reminded how Jesus used boats and fishing in his life and teachings, as in my first vision of Alex and my father at our Minnesota lake home. I consider my training as an engineer and am amazed that the Lord delivered his messages to me with order and crystal-clear understanding in a way that my personality type could comprehend. And there's the living reminder of my nephew Matt when he tells me that he talked with Ah-icks yet again.

God knows how to reach us. He's been initiating a connection with people from the early days of creation. I heard God's messages so clearly, but I've still wished to hear him louder, the way he communicated with Moses and Abraham.

But I suppose mature faith hears with the heart as well as with the ears, and I can take comfort that what he communicated to me was every bit as real as what he spoke to those ancient heroes. I can fortify my modern-day, real-time faith with the words of Exodus 20:22 and own the reminder that the God of time and eternity spoke to Moses: "The LORD said to Moses, '. . . You have seen for yourselves that I have talked with you from heaven'" (ESV).

Someone beyond myself met me at my most wounded. He met my son at his most wounded somewhere beyond this earth. If I can tell people about the wonderment of life and help anyone find hope for his or her sorrows and for the promise of a heavenly reunion someday, then maybe my journey through grief will make a shred of sense.

Through the most tragic event of my life, the Lord showed himself to me as he is—not as society or I have imagined him to be, not how we would like him to fit into a definition to suit our ways of thinking. He worked in me beyond my capabilities. He proved to me that he is Lord and I am not. He is the one with power and glory and control. And he proved that the reality of himself in the universe and in my personal life is a good thing, not confines to free myself from.

I was with Alex at the end of his life, as I had been with him at the beginning. The fact that he left me a message in the early hours, asking me to come down and help him, has alternately comforted and haunted me. But God has stepped in each time and stopped the tortured ruminations.

As my nurse friend Debi wrote in a sympathy note, the hole in my heart left from Alex's death will never go away or heal over completely. I will always bear a scar. But then she said that, although the bleeding artery in my heart would never evaporate, it would get smaller over time, through prayer and memories.

I have always detested the phrase "move on," because it suggests that we're supposed to forget about a great grief, as if we can just get over it. Trauma changes us; we are never the same. But the hope is that God will use everything, even something as tragic as suicide. My favorite condolence of all came from my own Jimmy, who wisely said, "Let's move *forward*, Pops. Let's take the high road."

In the years since Alex's passing, I have continued to feel as if I'm living between two worlds. Each day I have to remind myself multiple times that this season of missing him is temporary. I haven't really lost him. But for the rest of my life I will have to keep learning how to miss him and still go on with God's good purpose for my own life.

The remembrance of being on the bridge with Alex and the Trinity has sustained me through inevitable ups and downs triggered by his birthdays, holidays, or times when one of his friends has come over to check up on me.

I was given this gift of a final ten minutes with Alex, just the two of us along with our Healer.

I have been blessed to understand more fully the mysteries of this life and the assurances of the next one.

I have been carried by a God who is both mysterious Lord and familiar friend—and too nice a guy not to create an eternal reunion that will surpass everything of this life.

I have been given grace and the comprehension that all is well with my son and that he is waiting for the rest of us in our true home. I will hold him again, and we'll laugh together forever. But not yet. Not yet.

It's my hope that by writing down my recollection of that afternoon's events, Mindy, Bryan, Jimmy, my mom, siblings, other relatives, and countless others will receive a touch of the promises the Lord gave me to share.

Heaven is real and waiting for us all. I saw it, felt it, believe in it, and long for it. And so I wait for it.

In some ways, writing this book has been another vehicle to process, to embrace the pain. Having to replay the memories, going over the narrative, has been helpful even though very difficult. My counselor said it's necessary to fully feel the hurt in order for the entire wound to fully heal. I have certainly felt the hurt; I trust I am still healing.

Surprisingly, I have felt a zest return in putting my experiences on paper. Recalling God's messages to me in that Champaign condominium helps me focus on God's eternal plan, a plan that will wipe out all painful memories. If others can claim that hope for their own future reunions, then hallelujah and amen.

The unknowns of life still can trigger fear. Sometimes

heartache refuses to relent. But God is bigger and he is present. His presence is food that nourishes and heals me every day. For this new understanding, I am grateful, and I pray every day that I'll be the kind of Christian God uses, one he can be proud of.

A good friend worded her affirmation well after she heard me speak awhile back. She called me "the perfect messenger—an imperfect person delivering a beautiful lesson . . . from your mouth to God's ears, as well as [to] all of us who were present."

This understanding makes me want to be a better person and to turn my selfish attention over to him for remodeling, as I know I can't do it myself. I am strengthened by Alex's memory and by my Lord as I try to make up for lost time and become the person God created me to be.

And I now believe that sometime, someday, I will become that person, because I know I am not alone. I will see heaven in person.

In the meantime I will continue in this broken world, transformed by the hope of heaven.

Death Is Nothing at All

Death is nothing at all.
I have only slipped away into the next room.
I am I and you are you.
Whatever we were to each other

That we are still.
Call me by my old familiar name.
Speak to me in the easy way you always used.
Put no difference into your tone.
Wear no forced air of solemnity or sorrow.
Laugh as we always laughed
At the little jokes we always enjoyed together.
Play, smile, think of me, pray for me.
Let my name [Yalex!] be ever the household word that it
   always was.
Let it be spoken without effort
Without the ghost of a shadow in it.
Life means all that it ever meant.
It is the same as it ever was.
There is absolute unbroken continuity.
What is death but a neglible accident?
Why should I be out of mind
Because I am out of sight?
I am waiting for you for an interval
Somewhere very near
Just around the corner.
All is well.
Nothing is past, nothing is lost.
One brief moment and all will be as it was before.
How we shall laugh at the trouble of parting when we will
   meet again![14]

Notes

1. *Gladiator*, dir. Ridley Scott, 155 min., Dreamworks, 2003, DVD.
2. *Field of Dreams*, dir. Phil Alden Robinson, 106 min., Universal, 2012, DVD.
3. *Awakenings*, dir. Penny Marshall, 121 min., Columbia Pictures, 1990, VHS.
4. Catherine Woodiwiss, "A New Normal: Ten Things I've Learned about Trauma," God's Politics (blog), *Sojourners: Faith in Action for Social Justice*, January 13, 2014, http://sojo .net/blogs/2014/01/13/new-normal-ten-things-ive-learned -about-trauma/.
5. Josh Sanburn, "Suicide in America: The People Who Answer the Phone," *Time*, November 25, 2013, 64–65.
6. William Walsham How, "For all the saints, who from their labors rest," 1864.
7. Daniel L Schutte, "Here I Am, Lord," arranged by John Weissrock and Michael Pope, New Dawn Music/OCP Publications, 1981.
8. George Croly, "Spirit of God, descend upon my heart," Songs of Illumination, 1854.

9. Charles Wesley, "Love divine, all loves excelling, Joy of heaven, to earth come down," 1747.

10. Roy Rogers, feat. Dale Evans and The Whippoorwills, "Happy Trails," *Happy Trails: The Roy Rogers Collection*, 1937–1990, Disc 3, track 13, Rhino Entertainment, 1999, compact disc.

11. *Gladiator*, dir. Ridley Scott, 155 min., Dreamworks, 2003, DVD.

12. John F. Kennedy, American University Commencement Address, Washington, DC, June 10, 1963, http://www.american rhetoric.com/speeches/jfkamericanuniversityaddress.html.

13. John F. Kennedy, Inaugural Address, Washington, DC, January 20, 1961, www.pbs.org/wgbh/americanexperience /features/primary-resources/jfk-inaugural61/.

14. Canon Henry Scott Holland, "Death Is Nothing at All," (sermon, Westminster Abbey, London, England, 1910). Paraphrased version written to me in a three-page sympathy note by Hans Becherer, retired chairman of Deere and Co.

About the Authors

*A*lan M. Hallene Jr., PhD, is the father of three grown sons, one whom he anticipates reuniting with someday in heaven. While working on *The Hope of Heaven*, Al was on leave from his teaching position at St. Ambrose University in Davenport, Iowa. He has also taught at the University of Illinois and the University of Iowa, and is president of NorthHill Consulting, LLC.

*E*rin Keeley Marshall is the author of *Navigating Route 20-Something* and *The Daily God Book*. She spent the early years of her career as an editor at Tyndale House Publishers and has edited and written for several Christian publishing companies throughout the United States. She lives in Arkansas with her husband, Steve, and their two children.